STANDARDS FOR CATALOGING NONPRINT MATERIALS

FOURTH EDITION

AN INTERPRETATION AND PRACTICAL APPLICATION

Alma M. Tillin
Media Specialist
Berkeley Unified School District

and

William J. Quinly
Coordinator, Media Education
Instructional Design and Development
Florida State University

Published by
Association for Educational Communications and Technology
1201 Sixteenth Street, N.W.
Washington, D.C. 20036

Library of Congress Cataloging in Publication Data

Tillin, Alma M.
Standards for cataloging nonprint materials.

Edition for 1968, by NEA's Dept. of Audiovisual Instruction, published under title: Standards for cataloging, coding, and scheduling educational media; rev. ed. (1971) by the Cataloging Committee of the Association for Educational Communications and Technology; 3d ed. (1972) by the Information Science Committee of the Association for Educational Communications and Technology.
Bibliography: p.
Includes index.
1. Cataloging of non-book materials. I. Quinly, William J., joint author. II. Association for Educational Communications and Technology. Information Science Committee. Standards for cataloging nonprint materials. III. Title.
Z695.66.T54   1976   025.3'4'7   75-38605

AECT President, Harold Hill
AECT Executive Director, Howard Hitchens
AECT Director of Research and Communications, Clint J. Wallington
Production: Sandy M. Spicer
Editorial: Q. B. Monk

International Standard Book Number: 0-89240-000-5

Stock No. 071-02898

Additional copies of this book may be purchased by writing to the Publications Department, Association for Educational Communications and Technology, 1201 16th St., N.W., Washington, D.C. 20036

TABLE OF CONTENTS

Section One—Basic Cataloging Rules

Section Two—Cataloging of Specific Media

Appendices

DEDICATION

Mrs. Katharine W. Clugston, the most valued member of the team which prepared all previous editions of this manual, has retired from her position as Head of the Audiovisual Section, Descriptive Cataloging Division, Library of Congress. Her absence in this present effort is most keenly felt by the current authors.

Mrs. Clugston is an audiovisual cataloging authority without peer and her selfless devotion to the field has done much toward the establishment of cataloging standards. Her sage counsel and ready solutions to the most complex cataloging problems are most sorely missed.

It is to Mrs. Katharine W. Clugston that this volume is affectionately dedicated.

FOREWORD

The Association for Educational Communications and Technology has always recognized its obligation to the education, library, and information service community. One way in which it fulfills this obligation is by publishing materials—both print and nonprint—to serve the practitioners in this area. As the authors point out in their preface to this edition, AECT has pioneered in developing and publishing standards for cataloging nonprint materials.

As they have moved forward in this specialized area, the authors have also expanded the publication. This fourth edition of *Standards for Cataloging Nonprint Materials* is far more detailed and offers many more examples than the previous edition. This was done in response to feedback from those who used the previous edition. AECT and the authors have been particularly sensitive to user needs as well as to various standards proposed by other groups.

Alma Tillin and William Quinly, the authors of this edition, have brought their expertise and experience to bear in developing a manual which will undoubtedly be a new benchmark in the cataloging of nonprint media. I wish to extend to them my personal thanks and the deep appreciation of the Association and its members for their successful completion of a difficult task. It is the efforts of such dedicated people that make AECT a successful association.

Howard Hitchens
Executive Director
January, 1976

PREFACE TO THE FOURTH EDITION

The Association for Educational Communications and Technology (formerly the Department of Audiovisual Instruction) was the first national professional organization to develop coding and cataloging rules for nonprint media. As the result of the work of a task force organized in 1966 by Dr. Anna L. Hyer, then executive secretary of DAVI, the *Standards for Cataloging, Coding and Scheduling Educational Media* was published in 1968.

Other organizations have since become actively concerned with the problems of nonbook cataloging, and liaison has been established with the Educational Media Producers Council, the Library of Congress, appropriate committees of the American, Canadian, and British Library Associations, and the National Council for Educational Technology.

The first revision of these rules was published in 1971 as the *Standards for Cataloging Nonprint Materials.* The 1971 edition was devoted exclusively to cataloging standards since the coding for many of the nonprint formats had been included in the Library of Congress MARC System. (See *Films: A MARC Format,* Library of Congress, 1970, and supplements to date.) The second revision was published in 1971, and the third edition in 1972.

During the interval since the first publication there have been numerous conferences, meetings, and books on nonprint cataloging. AECT, ALA, and CLA formed the Joint Committee on Cataloging Nonbook Materials, which advised on the content of the Canadian Library Association publication *Non-book Materials: The Organization of Integrated Collections.* The Baker & Taylor Company funded the Task Force on Nonprint Media Guidelines, chaired by Pearce S. Grove. The British Library Association Media Cataloging Rules Committee published its work, *Non-book Materials Cataloging Rules,* in 1973.

With the recent completion of the interim revision of Chapter 12, AACR, the Library of Congress proposed solutions to a number of the outstanding differences existing among the several publications. There is not yet, however, complete agreement on every facet of nonbook cataloging. This volume attempts to reflect what the authors consider to be the thinking of the majority of those who have participated with them in the various discussions.

It has become evident from the questions, comments, and discussions that all those involved in providing access to nonprint media wish to be kept informed about the latest developments in cataloging standards. They also seek guidance in synthesizing existing and proposed rules into a practical instrument for immediate use. Numerous requests have been received for examples which demonstrate how the rules can be interpreted in cataloging all types of nonprint media as well as in handling problems specific to each type of material. The need for additional information on the coding of nonprint media has also been indicated.

The media code developed for use in computerized retrieval systems by the Task Force on Nonprint Media Guidelines, in cooperation with the National Audiovisual Center, has been included with minor modifications in the appendices to this volume.

No set of cataloging rules should be considered absolute as long as there are innovations in technology and new materials are introduced in various formats. The purpose of these rules is to state certain basic premises which can be used as guides. This purpose is defeated if the rules are stated so inflexibly that they cannot incorporate the changes demanded by current conditions or if the rules are interpreted as inflexible and followed with such rigidity that the practitioner cannot cope with change. The intent in this work, therefore, is to present the rules in a manner that will facilitate their understanding, and to demonstrate by numerous examples how they may be flexibly interpreted in practical application. Since the real test of cataloging standards is their application in a wide variety of situations, comments from those using this manual are solicited.

Alma M. Tillin

William J. Quinly

ACKNOWLEDGMENTS

We are deeply indebted to the many persons who have contributed directly and indirectly to this volume. Special acknowledgment is given to the members of the original AECT Cataloging Committee whose contributions laid the foundation for this edition: Mrs. Katharine W. Clugston, now retired from the Library of Congress; Ford Lemler of the University of Michigan; and Robert Hayes of the Scott Education Division who represented the Educational Media Producers Council.

Several specialists in cataloging and technology contributed their expertise. The reports and position papers of John Byrum of Princeton University and the American Library Association Subcommittee on Rules for Cataloging Machine-Readable Data Files, and the suggestions of Henriette Avram of the Library of Congress, Elizabeth Herman of the University of California, Los Angeles, and Howard Huff of the Florida State University were invaluable in writing the section on machine-readable data file. Our thanks also go to Benny Tucker and Vivian Schrader of the Library of Congress, Jerome K. Miller of the University of Illinois, and Suzanne Massonneau of Texas A & M University who provided constructive criticism of the entire volume.

Colleagues in libraries and educational technology were consulted frequently and their suggestions are incorporated throughout the book. Special appreciation is expressed to the members of the Institute on Systems and Standards for the Bibliographic Control of Media, the Nonprint Media Guidelines Task Force, and the Joint Advisory Committee on Nonbook Materials for their contributions. There were also many interesting exchanges with our British friends, Antony Croghan, Bernard Chibnall, and Peter Lewis.

Lastly, we appreciate the fortitude of our respective families, our editors, and of our colleagues who waited patiently as we continued to revise and update this edition long past several deadlines.

INTRODUCTION

The need for cataloging standards is expressed in the introduction to the *Anglo-American Cataloging Rules*, prepared by the American Library Association, the Library of Congress, the Library Association, and the Canadian Library Association. There is a "...manifest general need, permeating all library, bibliographical, and . . . trade activities, for a standard mode of identifying bibliographical entities. Such standard identification is of great importance in (multiple-entry catalogs), single-entry bibliographies, book (and nonbook) lists, order lists, bibliographical citations, and everyday communications referring to bibliographical entities."*

The approved cataloging principles stated in the *Anglo-American Cataloging Rules* provide the instrument for accomplishing this needed standardization, and should be used as the basic guide in cataloging audiovisual materials. In using the AACR, attention is called to the importance of consulting the latest rule revisions that have been incorporated into the code since its publication in 1967. All references to AACR rules 130-153 cited in this work are from the revised edition of Chapter 6.†

Elaboration of these rules and suggestions for variations to meet the needs of different media centers are brought out in this handbook. These rules should be regarded as provisional, especially those regarding the newer types of media, until procedures have been tested and cataloging rules have been adopted by groups concerned with the utilization of the various media.

The terms *nonprint, nonbook,* and *audiovisual* are used interchangeably to designate all materials that are not in the traditional book format. The rules are not designed to cover manuscripts or music, nor ephemeral material such as newspaper clippings and illustrative material of various sorts which are of temporary value and do not merit full cataloging. Such materials are usually arranged according to their general subject content and stored in folders or vertical files.

In Section One, the basic cataloging rules that apply to all types of nonprint materials are presented. They cover all the elements that may be needed to identify, describe, and retrieve a work. The extent

---

**Anglo-American Cataloging Rules; North American Text,* ed. by C. Sumner Spaulding. Chicago: American Library Association, 1967, p. 2.

†*Anglo-American Cataloging Rules, North American Text: Chapter 6, Separately Published Monographs.* Chicago: American Library Association, 1974.

of the information and description that appears on the catalog card or in the book catalog will vary in accordance with the needs of the clientele of each media center and with the special purpose for which the catalog is compiled, e.g., a catalog of 16mm motion pictures available for rental. To aid in determining which descriptive details are needed for small, medium, and large resource centers, the primary purpose of the various elements in the cataloging record is indicated. In the examples provided to clarify various rules, abbreviations and punctuation are the same as those used in the sample catalog cards in Section Two.

In Section Two, the cataloging rules are applied to specific media. For each type of material, sample cards illustrate cataloging that ranges from the fully descriptive to the very simplified. Cards are included to demonstrate how to handle some of the particular problems that may occur.

This is not a manual on how to catalog. It is assumed that those who use it have a knowledge of cataloging, classification, and subject analysis. References to the *Anglo-American Cataloging Rules* are provided to assist those who wish to consult the full text of the original rule. This volume concerns itself solely with the cataloging of nonprint materials. Those desiring guidance in the establishment of resource centers and their operation should consult the works listed in the bibliography on page 225.

SECTION ONE
BASIC CATALOGING RULES

I. CATALOG ELEMENTS

Cataloging provides a means of gaining access to knowledge resources by identifying, describing, and organizing them for ready retrieval. The information given includes elements of identification, description, and organization. The elements are grouped by type in the following summary. A full discussion of each element will be found under its appropriate heading.

A. Elements of Identification.

The elements of identification supply information to identify a work and to distinguish it from any other work. For audiovisual materials, the elements of identification include:

1. Title
2. Medium designator
3. Creator(s)—author(s), artist(s), composer(s), director(s), performer(s), scriptwriter(s), consultant(s), and others who have contributed to the work
4. Edition
5. Producer/Sponsor
6. Date
7. Physical description—specific type of material; distinguishing physical characteristics, e.g., 8mm or 16mm, sound or silent, etc.
8. Standard numbering (SN)

B. Elements of Description

The elements of description furnish information concerning the nature and scope of a work and its bibliographical history and relationships. For audiovisual materials the elements of description include:

1. Place of producer and distributor
2. Distributor
3. Physical description (other than identifying characteristics)
4. Series and subseries
5. Notes (including educational level)

C. Elements of Organization

The elements of organization provide an analysis of the work and a means for its retrieval. For audiovisual materials the elements of organization include:

1. Main entry
2. Uniform title
3. Tracings
4. Classification number
5. Media code

All elements in each category may not be applicable in every instance. Additions and/or deletions may be necessary to meet the requirements of the catalog users. Before excluding an item, the cataloger should consider the potential growth of the collection and the difficulty involved in accumulating the information at some later date. Resource centers which participate in cooperative or inter-library network arrangements may need to add the name or identification code of the center holding certain titles, such as the Standard Account Number (SAN).

In catalogs limited to a specific medium, those elements which are common to all entries in the catalog may be omitted, e.g., in a printed catalog listing only 16mm sound motion pictures in color, the medium designator, color, sound, and size notations would be omitted. Some catalogs may require the inclusion of variable information such as rental rates, purchase price, shelf numbers, etc.

II. ARRANGEMENT OF THE CATALOG ELEMENTS

The elements of catalog data are organized by prescribed areas which may contain one or several elements. Areas and elements are indicated by specified punctuation. The punctuation prescribed in the *ISBD(M)—International Standard Bibliographic Description for Monographic Publications* is given on page 32. In the cataloging examples in Section Two, this punctuation has been adapted for nonprint works and condensed for the typewritten card.

The elements are arranged in the following order (see also Section Two, Arrangement of Elements on the Catalog Card, p. 30):

Area 1. MAIN ENTRY
Entry under:
A. Title (p. 4)
B. Series Title (p. 5)
C. Creator (p. 6)

Area 2. TITLE/MEDIUM DESIGNATOR/STATEMENT OF CREATOR RESPONSIBILITY
- Title. If title main entry is used, the title is not repeated.
- Medium Designator
- Statement of Creator Responsibility

Area 3. EDITION
- Edition statement
- Statement of creator responsibility for the edition

Area 4. IMPRINT
- Place
- Producer or Publisher/Sponsor/Distributor
- Date. Copyright, production, release date.

Area 5. COLLATION
- Physical Description. Various elements.

Area 6. SERIES
- Series Title. If series title main entry is used, the series title is not repeated.
- Number Within the Series
- Subseries
- Number Within the Subseries

Area 7. NOTES
- Educational Level
- Extension of Physical Description
- Accompanying and/or Descriptive Material
- Other Versions
- Title. Source of title; title variations
- Related Works
- Credits
- Summary
- Contents

Area 8. OTHER IDENTIFYING AND ORGANIZATIONAL DATA
- Standard Numbering (SN)
- Tracings
- Classification Number
- Media Code
- Additional Information

III. SOURCE OF INFORMATION

In general, except for the medium designator, the items in the title, edition, and series area represent the information on the work itself. The medium designator and the collation are a description of the physical work, and should be derived from an inspection whenever possible. Information and description in Areas 1-6 are expressed in standard bibliographical and technical terminology. "The rest of the description consists of statements quoted from the work or from other sources, of statements phrased by the cataloger, or of a combination of the two if this results in the clearest and most concise statement."*

The information given in the various areas of the catalog entry are taken from the following sources, listed in the preferred order of use:

1. The material itself, including the container when the container is an integral part of the item, e.g., a cassette or cartridge.
2. Accompanying data, i.e., guides, notes, and other leaflets issued with the item.
3. Producer's data, i.e., catalogs and other promotional brochures.
4. The container, when it is completely separate from the work itself, e.g., 16mm reel can, audiorecording container, various other storage cases.
5. Other sources, e.g., reference works, indexes, etc.

The compilation of complete data may necessitate a search of all the sources applicable to the particular material, and in many instances, conflicting information may be found. As a general rule, the authenticity of information should be determined on the basis of the priority order of the source. Specific rules on sources are given in the discussion of the various catalog elements, and in Section Two which deals separately with each type of material.

IV. MAIN ENTRY (Area 1)

Main entry may be made under title, series title, or creator.

A. Title Main Entry

Title main entry is usually preferred for nonbook media. Printed materials have traditionally been entered under the name of the person or corporate body (designated as the author) chiefly responsible for the intellectual and artistic content of the work. Audiovisual media

---

**Anglo-American Cataloging Rules, North American Text: Chapter 6, Separately Published Monographs.* Chicago; American Library Association, 1974, p. 6.

are deemed to be an exception to this general rule because the majority of them are created by collaborative effort. The difficulty in establishing that the overall responsibility for the whole of the work can be attributed to one person makes an author entry inappropriate. Since most audiovisual productions are known only by title and are primarily cited by title in the trade and reference sources, a main entry under a name that has little significance in the identification of the work should be avoided. For example, the script writer and editor of American Landmark audiorecordings is Elise Bell. Since she is rarely associated with the titles of the works in the series, her name should not be used for main entry. An added entry may be made for Elise Bell, if desired.

Title main entry preferred:
The California gold rush. [Audiorecording]

Personal name main entry not recommended:
Bell, Elise
The California gold rush. [Audiorecording]

B. Series Title Main Entry

As a general rule, separate works that comprise a series or set should each be cataloged under its own title. In certain instances, however, it is advisable to use the series title for the main entry, and to consider the title of each individual item as a subtitle of the series title. Although the decision to use the series title for the main entry may be dictated by several different factors, it usually occurs under one of the following conditions:

1. Subject interrelationship. The series title may be used for the main entry when the subject matter of the individual items is so closely interrelated that, in essence, each is a part of the whole subject. This is especially evident when the individual title is of such a general nature that it conveys no specific meaning unless it is used in conjunction with the series title, or explanatory words are supplied.

Individual title: Geographic areas.
Series title: People and geography of South America.
Series title main entry:
People and geography of South America: Geographic areas. [Filmstrip]

2. Availability of individual items. If the various items in a series are not available as separate works because they are sold by the producer only as a complete set, the series title is the identifying element that is used for the main entry. Added entries or analytics may be made for the subjects and/or titles of the individual items.

3. Separate audio medium. When the audio accompaniment is not an integral part of the work, but is provided in a separate medium which is designed to accompany more than one individual item, e.g., two or more filmstrips with one audiorecording, the series title main entry obviates the difficulty of establishing which of the several individual titles included in the audio accompaniment should be used as the main entry. Added entries may be made for the individual titles if they are distinctive.

C. Creator Main Entry

The term *creator* designates the author, artist, photographer, composer, performer, producer, director, scriptwriter, consultant, or any other person who has made a significant contribution to the creation of the work. Although performers, producers, directors, consultants, designers, etc. have traditionally been excluded from consideration insofar as main entry is concerned, their importance in creating the work should be judged in relation to the nature and purpose of the particular medium. They may perform functions that are different from the accepted ones of author, composer, or artist, but they are, nevertheless, essential in the creation of a work in an audiovisual medium. They should, therefore, be considered for creator main entry.

1. Original works. An original work in an audiovisual medium for which the primary intellectual and artistic responsibility can be clearly established may be entered under the creator. An added entry is made for the title.

Evans, Bergen
The Bergen Evans vocabulary program. [Filmstrip]

Beswick, John S.
The Language of color. [Filmstrip] Compiled, photographed, and annotated by John S. Beswick.

2. Reproductions. An audiovisual work which is an *exact* reproduction of a printed work that would be cataloged under author may be entered in the same manner as the original work, e.g., a filmstrip reproduction of a picture book, a microfiche of a book. If the exactness of the reproduction is in doubt, and a lengthy comparison would be required for verification, the audiovisual work is entered under title, and an added entry is made for the author.

An exact reproduction of a picture book:
Johnson, Crockett
A picture for Harold's room. [Filmstrip]

Based on the picture book:
A Picture for Harold's room by Crockett Johnson. [Filmstrip]
(The author's name appears as part of the title on the audiovisual work. See Basic Rule V.A6, p. 8.)

A motion picture adapted from the book:
A Picture for Harold's room by Crockett Johnson. [Motion picture]
Adapted and directed by Gene Deitch.

A reproduction of a work originally produced in a nonbook medium is entered in the same manner as the original, e.g., a slide or transparency of a work of art; a sound recording of a script or captions from a filmstrip.

Reproduction of a painting:
Picasso, Pablo
Guernica. [Slide]

3. Dramatizations, abridgments, adaptations. An audiovisual work that is a dramatization, abridgment, or adaptation of an original printed work is entered under title.

Captains courageous. [Audiorecording]
A dramatization with music and sound effects based on the book of the same title by Rudyard Kipling.

It may be entered under the author of the original work if the purpose of the library is best served by keeping together all formats in which the title has been reproduced, e.g., in a school media center where book and audiovisual formats of a work are used together to improve reading skills.

Kipling, Rudyard
Captains courageous. [Audiorecording]
A dramatization with music and sound effects.

V. TITLE/MEDIUM DESIGNATOR/STATEMENT OF CREATOR RESPONSIBILITY (Area 2)

A. Title

The title selected for the catalog entry will be the one which appears on the material itself.

1. Alternate source of title. If the material does not provide adequate information regarding the title, it may be taken from accompanying data such as the teacher's guide or lecture notes, the producer's catalogs, the container, or other reference sources. (See Basic Rule III, p. 4.)

2. Transcription of title. The title should be transcribed exactly as it appears as to wording and spelling. Long Title statements may be abridged as long as the shortened title retains the first several words of the original title, and there is no loss of essential information. All omissions are indicated by ellipses (. . .). The full title may be given in a note.

The *Anglo-American Cataloging Rules*, with its current revisions, should be used as a guide for punctuation, capitalization, correction of obvious spelling errors, romanization of title, use of Arabic and Roman numerals, etc. Certain adaptations of these rules may be necessitated by such factors as the specialized nature of the catalog, the particular audience, or the limitations inherent in a manual or automated system. For example, the cataloger may elect to drop the article at the beginning of the title, or to follow accepted English language rules for capitalization and punctuation. If adaptations are made, they should be carried out consistently throughout the entire catalog.

3. Variations in title. If more than one title appears on the work, preference is given the title closest to the subject content of the work. When such a sequence does not exist, the title most prominently displayed is used. If there are variations in the the title used on the work, the producer's or publisher's catalogs, or the container, the variations are cited in a note if the work may be known by these titles. Added entries may be made for variant title(s) if they are judged to be significant in identifying the work.

4. Supplied title. If no title appears on the work, and no authoritative title is found in the reference sources, a title is supplied by the cataloger and is shown in brackets (*AACR*, 134B5).

[Human heart] [Transparency]

5. Meaningless title. Titles which are by themselves meaningless may be expanded by the use of additional words supplied by the cataloger and shown in brackets, as long as the first word or words are those of the original title.

Introduction [to Florida wildlife] [Filmstrip]

6. Creator's name as part of the title. If the title includes the name of the creator, producer, etc., and for linguistic or other reasons must be regarded as an integral part of the title, it is so transcribed.

Walt Disney's Story of Pinocchio. [Filmstrip]

a. *Name of the creator of the original work as part of the title of the reproduction.* If the name of the author, artist, composer, etc., of the original work appears as part of the title on the reproduction in another medium, it is so transcribed.

Marchesa Balbi [by] Van Dyck. [Picture]
Shakespeare's Julius Caesar. [Motion picture]
Finlandia and Valse triste by Jean Sibelius. [Filmstrip]

7. Uniform title. A uniform title may be required in some catalogs to bring together the entries for all of the titles by which the work is known. This consists essentially of the title under which the work was originally issued, or alternatively, the title by which the work is most often cited in the literature (*AACR*, Chapter 4, and rules 233-243).

Beethoven, Ludwig van
[Mass, op. 123, D major] [Audiorecording]
Missa solemnis in D, for four solo voices . . . op. 123.

8. Change in title. When the title of a work is changed, with or without a change in content, this fact is given in a note. An added entry may be made for the earlier title.

9. Subtitle. The main title is frequently supplemented by an explanatory subtitle. If the subtitle is sufficiently brief, it should be included in the Title statement immediately following the main title. If the subtitle is of such length that it would cause the medium designator to be so far down on the card that it would be less than readily apparent, the subtitle should be given in a note.

Short subtitle retained after the main title:

The Pleasure is mutual: how to conduct effective picture book programs. [Motion picture]

Long subtitle which should be included in a note:

Plows, cultivators, planters, seeders, grain harvesters, and threshing machines; the history and development of agricultural implements and machinery from 1850 to the early part of the twentieth century. [Filmstrip]

The subtitle may be omitted if it is not essential to the meaning of the main title.

10. Works in parts. If a work has been divided into parts, and each part has been identified separately, the designation and title of the part are included in the title proper.

The ABC of puppet making. Part 1. [Motion picture]
Doing geometry. Part 1, Points, lines and planes. [Audiorecording]

If the entry includes more than one part, e.g., Part 1, Part 2, and each has a different title, the designation and the title of each part is given in the Contents note.

B. Medium Designator

Medium designators are used to distinguish one type of physical format from another. Medium designators are either *general physical form designators* which indicate the basic format of the material, or *specific physical form designators* which provide a more exact identification of the format, alerting the user to the possible need for special equipment in order to utilize the item.

1. General physical form designator. The general medium designator *(medium designator)* is always given in the singular form (except Realia) immediately following the full title, and is usually enclosed in square brackets. Square brackets indicate that the information is supplied by the cataloger. They may be omitted, if desired, since the position of the medium designator is established in the catalog record. The purpose of the medium designator is to notify the user briefly and immediately of the general medium in which the work appears. Those users interested in this format will read further for more detail, while those who are not interested will pass on to the next listing. (For medium designators in added entries see Basic Rule XI.B2, p. 25.)

The use of medium designators, i.e., general designators, will prevent the proliferation of media designators, a hazard associated with the use of specific designators, and will at the same time be hospitable to further developments in the various types of media.

The following medium designators are used:

Audiorecording
Chart
Diorama
Filmstrip
Flash card
Game
Globe
Kit
Machine-readable data file
Map
Microform
Model
Motion picture
Picture
Realia
Slide
Transparency
Videorecording

The medium designator of the dominant medium is used for works containing dependent and/or accompanying media, which are listed in the Collation or in a note. For example, a filmstrip and an audiorecording which explains the pictures of the filmstrip are cataloged as a filmstrip; an audiorecording and a filmstrip which visually illustrates the sound are cataloged as an audiorecording.

A package of materials in more than one medium, designed for use as a unit and containing no one medium so clearly dominant that the others are dependent or accompanying, is cataloged as a kit. The *principal* components of a kit may be of sufficient significance that, if desired, they can be entered in the catalog as analytics or as separately cataloged entities. The medium designator "Kit" applies also to a collection in only one medium when the materials are specifically designed and coordinated to be used according to a prescribed method (e.g., a programed instruction kit) or for a particular purpose (e.g., a laboratory kit).

2. Specific physical form designator. The specific physical form designator *(specific designator)* is given in the Collation (Physical Description). Its purpose is to further refine the physical characteristics and functions of the medium.

In the following listing, specific designators for formats that are currently in use are shown with their medium designators. For some media, specific designators for archival and/or experimental formats or other peculiarities (see Machine-readable data file) are grouped separately. The list, while comprehensive, does not pretend to be all-inclusive. Omitted are formats that are essentially curiosities, such as a music box, and many that are considered archival or experimental. As the latter are developed and utilized more widely, other specific designators may be added, for example, the integram which is a hologram of moving objects produced without laser illumination. Caution should be exercised, however, in adopting new terms. In establishing the terminology of new designators, it is essential to differentiate between the trade name of a "new" format and its actual physical characteristics. In some instances the format may already be adequately described by some existing designator even though the format is represented as new when produced under a different name.

Depending upon the specificity of physical form required by the user, and the size of the collection, the cataloger may elect to use a term that combines the physical characteristics that are described by two different specific designators. For example, "relief map" (or chart) and "wall map" (or chart) may also be a "relief wall map" (or chart). It is recommended, however, that the addition of such terms be kept to a minimum and that, in such instances, the specific designator be used that describes the physical characteristics judged to be the most useful for the particular audience. The other physical characteristic would then be described in a note. In an elementary school, for example, the specific designator "relief map", with a note "A wall map", would be more significant for instructional purposes than the specific designator "wall map", with a note "A relief map".

The specific designators *cartridge, cassette, disc,* and *reel* are common to several different media. When these specific designators are used out of context with their medium designators, an ambiguity in medium may occur. For example, a work in one medium may include a separate dependent work in another medium, such as a filmstrip with an audio accompaniment. Or, the specific designator may be required in an identifying or descriptive statement in which there is no reference to its medium designator. In such cases, the combining form of the medium designator is added to the specific designator to identify the medium, e.g., audiocassette, microcassette, videocassette; audiodisc, videodisc; audioreel, microreel, videoreel, etc. If there is no combining form in the medium designator, the medium designator itself or an equivalent descriptor is used in conjunction with the specific designator, e.g., motion picture reel, motion picture cartridge, digital disc (for machine-readable data file).

MEDIUM DESIGNATOR	SPECIFIC DESIGNATOR
Audiorecording	Cartridge Cassette Disc Reel Roll
Archival/Experimental	Cylinder Page Wire
Chart	Chart Flannel board set Flip chart Graph Magnetic board set Relief chart Wall chart
Diorama	Diorama
Filmstrip	Filmslip Filmstrip
Flash card	Card
Game	Game Puzzle Simulation
Globe	Globe Relief globe
Kit	Exhibit Kit Laboratory kit Programed instruction kit
Machine-readable data file	
Species of file	Data file Program file
Storage medium	Disc Punched card Punched paper tape Tape
Map	Map Relief map Wall map

Microform	Aperture card Card Cartridge Cassette Fiche Reel Ultrafiche
Model	Mock-up Model
Motion picture	Cartridge Cassette Loop Reel
Picture	Art original Art print Hologram Photograph Picture Post card Poster Stereograph Study print
Realia	Name of object Specimen
Slide	Audioslide Microscope slide Slide Stereoscope slide
Transparency	Transparency
Videorecording	Cartridge Cassette Disc Reel

C. Statement of Creator Responsibility

If the work is entered under the name of a creator, the function(s) performed and the name are recorded after the medium designator in the statement of creator responsibility.

Radlauer, Edward
  Custom cars. [Filmstrip] Written and photographed by Ed Radlauer.

The statement includes the names of joint creators if there is a shared responsibility in the performance of the same function(s).

> Nolan, Mary Lee
> Indian Mexico: Heritage of the past. [Filmstrip] Produced, written, and photographed by Mary Lee Nolan and Sidney Nolan.

If the work is not entered under the name of a creator, persons who are primarily responsible for the creation of the work and are *significant in its identification* may be named in the statement of creator responsibility. If there is doubt that the names are essential for the identification of the work, the statement of creator responsibility is omitted, and the names are given in the notes area, as appropriate.

As a general rule, the statement of creator responsibility is transcribed as found in the formal statement in the work. However, where multiple functions and names are involved, changes may be made in grouping functions and names if less repetition and a briefer statement of creator responsibility will result. Names of persons performing the same function are separated by commas; names of persons performing different functions are separated by semicolons.

> Language development. [Motion picture] Director, Glen Howard; authors, Jerome Kagan, Howard Gardner.

If more than three names are listed for any one function, only the name cited first is given, followed by the phrase "and others."

> Some haystacks don't even have a needle and other complete modern poems. [Audiorecording] Compiled by Stephen Dunning, and others.

VI. EDITION (Area 3)

A. Edition

When a work is revised in the same medium, the revised work is referred to as a new edition. If there is no change in title, a simple statement, e.g., 2d ed., Rev. ed., according to the wording on the work itself, is inserted after the medium designator.

> American flag. [Motion picture] 2d ed.

If there is a change in title, the edition statement is omitted. Information regarding change in title, date, and other relationships of the various editions is given in a note. Added entries should be made for the title of earlier editions which are in the collection.

> Revised version of 1972 motion picture entitled Visualization—key to reading.

> Revised version of 1965 transparency set of the same title.

B. Statement of Creator Responsibility for the Edition

When the revision is the work of someone other than the creator of the original edition, a brief statement of creator responsibility is given following the Edition statement. When edition details are given in a note, creator responsibility for the edition is included. An added entry may be made for the creator of the edition.

VII. IMPRINT (Area 4)

The imprint consists of the following elements: *place* (the city of the principal offices of the producer/publisher, and of the distributor, if other than the producer; *name* of the producer/publisher, of the sponsor (if any), and of the distributor; and *date* of copyright/production and/or release.

A. Place

Give the city of the producer's or publisher's, and distributor's principal offices. Place is not given for a sponsor. If the place is obscure and it is necessary to identify it or distinguish it from another place of the same name, add the name of the state (if in the U.S.) or the name of the country (if outside the U.S.). Abbreviations of State names recommended by the U.S. Postal Service are used (see Appendix IV).*

New York: Texture Films

Burlingame, CA: Lee Mendelson Film Productions

Amersham, Eng.: Hulton Educational Publications

London: Common Ground, 1957; Pine Grove, Canada: Distributed by Carman Educational Associates, 1966

New York: NBC; Wilmette, IL: Released by Films Incorporated, 1971.

If the location is unknown, record the probable place followed by a question mark, the whole enclosed within brackets.

Basic musical forms. [Transparency] [Atlanta?]: Bassett Publications, 1974.

If the place cannot be conjectured, the abbreviation "[s.l.]" (i.e., sine loco) is used.

---

*The ALA Catalog Code Revision Committee has reversed it's decision to use the U.S. Postal Service State abbreviations and is now recommending that the list as given in the current AACR (Mass., Conn., etc.) be used in the second edition.

Because producers, publishers, and distributors frequently change the location of their offices, many catalogers omit place from the public catalog card and record it only as accession information on the shelf list card, except where the producer and/or distributor is located in a country other than that of the cataloging agency.

B. Producer/Sponsor/Distributor

1. Producer. A producer is defined as the company, institution, organization, or individual who determines the content and form of the material, and is responsible for its manufacture or production. The location and name(s) of the producer(s) are given first in the Imprint statement. The name(s) of the producer(s) already cited in the Statement of creator responsibility need not be repeated unless there is no other producer, publisher, or distributor responsible for issuing the work.

2. Sponsor. A sponsor is defined as the company, institution, organization, or individual other than the producer who finances the production of the material. Sponsorship often involves the promotion, either directly or indirectly, of a product or point of view. The name(s) of the sponsor(s) is recorded second in the Imprint statement, preceded by the phrase "sponsored by." The qualification as to function is always given when producer and sponsor are different. However, if one entity is responsible for both production and sponsorship, it is treated as the producer and no statement of sponsorship is necessary. Location is not noted for sponsors. A semicolon is used to separate the names of producer and sponsor.

Chicago: Sears, Roebuck and Co.; sponsored by the Joint Council on Economic Education.

3. Distributor. A distributor is defined as the organization which has exclusive national distribution rights for the work. Any sales organization which does not meet this definition should be considered as a regional or nonexclusive purchase source, and should not qualify as a distributor. The location and name of the distributor are recorded third in the Imprint statement. The phrase "Distributed by" or "Released by" is used after the location to indicate that the availability source is other than the producer. Since the name of the distributor is always placed after that of the producer, the qualification as to function for the distributor may be omitted, if desired.

Producer/Sponsor/Distributor

Chicago: Sears, Roebuck and Co.; sponsored by the Joint Council on Economic Education; New York: Released by Association-Sterling Films, 1972.

Producer/Distributor

London: BBC-TV; New York: Released by Time-Life Films, 1971.

If information on producer/sponsor/distributor is lacking, the abbreviation "[s.n.]" (i.e., sine nomine) is used. The absence of information on both place and producer/sponsor/distributor is indicated by "[s.l.; s.n.]".

4. Form of entry. The names of the companies are given in the briefest form by which they can be positively identified. Standard abbreviations such as Co., Dept., are used, and the terms of incorporation are omitted (*AACR*, 138) except where they are an integral part of the name, e.g., Films Incorporated. Initialisms may be substituted for company names if they will be understood by the catalog user (*AACR*, 138C, D).

BFA	for BFA Educational Media
EBEC	for Encyclopaedia Britannica Educational Corporation
IFB	for International Film Bureau, Incorporated

C. Date (Copyright, production, release)

1. Copyright date. The copyright date indicates the year in which authorized copies of a work are first made available to the public, either by sale or by other methods of distribution. The copyright date must appear on the work itself and is preceded by the copyright symbol "©", except on audiorecordings for which the copyright symbol is "℗".

2. Production date. The production date is interpreted as the date of copyright unless there appears on the work itself both a copyright date and a date which indicates that the work was completed, but not made available to the public, at a date other than that of the copyright. When the only date on the work appears without a copyright symbol, it is interpreted as the production date.

3. Release date. The release date is the year in which a work becomes available for wide distribution, usually through an established agency. In general, the copyright and release date are the same. In some instances they may differ, however, as when only a limited number of copies of a work are made available at the time of copyright and a channel and copies for general distribution are not provided until a later date. For example, a one-man producer may copyright his work when he produces it, but he may not make arrangements for its marketing until a year or more after the copyright is registered.

The release date is recorded only if it differs from the copyright date. Differences occur most frequently in foreign productions which may not be distributed in the country of the cataloging agency until a later date.

4. Notation of date. A date is always given in the Imprint statement, the latest copyright date taking preference over all other dates. If the number of dates that appear on a work are so numerous that recording them all in the Imprint statement would cause confusion, the dates in excess of those required in the Imprint, as explained in the preceding sections, may be given in a note if the publication history of the work is considered important.

The copyright date, preceded by "c" is given for all works (including audiorecordings)* following the name of the producer, e.g., EBEC, c1974, or following the name of the distributor when there is both a producer and a distributor.

> Montreal: National Film Board of Canada; New York: Distributed by Donars, c1973.

When both a copyright and a production date appear on the work, the copyright date only need be recorded. When the copyright and production date differ, the production date may be shown parenthetically after the copyright date, e.g., c1971 (1969). When a production date (i.e., a date without the copyright symbol) is the only one on the work, the copyright designator "c" is omitted from the notation.

If the date of release is significantly different from the date of copyright, it is recorded after the copyright date and is preceded by the word "released".

Copyright, release date
McGraw-Hill, c1949; released 1952.

Production, release date
Massachusetts Council for the Humanities, 1969; released 1973.

If there is both a producer and distributor, and the date of release by the distributor is significantly different from the copyright/production date, the copyright/production date is given after the producer, and the release date after the distributor.

> Montreal: National Film Board of Canada, c1970; New York: Distributed by Donars, 1972.

If neither the copyright/production or release date can be established, a probable date of production should be shown in brackets.

---

*For audiorecordings, the interim revision of Chapter 14 of the AACR uses "p" preceding the copyright date.

[1968?]	Probable date
[ca. 1915]	Approximate date
[196-]	Decade certain
[196-?]	Decade uncertain
[1966 or 7]	One of two years certain

The abbreviation "n.d." signifying no indication of date should not be used.

VIII. COLLATION (PHYSICAL DESCRIPTION) (Area 5)

The Collation presents the physical description of the work. The nature of most nonbook materials makes immediate access and inspection difficult, so the description provided should be sufficiently complete to identify the work, to distinguish it from all other versions of the same work, and to guide the user in the selection of any equipment which may be necessary to utilize the material. The physical description should be derived from an inspection or previewing of the item whenever possible. The amount of detail included will depend upon the nature of the resource center.

The physical description should include the following items, as applicable. It should be understood that not every medium will include all of the following items. For specific details see Collation of works in each medium in Section II, and the Physical Description Chart, Appendix I.

A. Number of Items and Specific Designator (including diameter of discs, reels)
B. Physical Contents
C. Length (playing time, number of frames, etc.)
D. Sound Statement
E. Color Statement
F. Size (width of tape, film; height, width, depth dimensions)
G. Playback Speed
H. Recording Mode
I. Accompaniments (audio, other)
J. Other Physical Characteristics

Metric measurement is preferred. However, until the conversion is well understood, the size of tapes, reels, discs, and slides is shown in inches on the sample cards in Section II. Audiotape playback speed is also shown in inches per second (ips). The metric equivalent is given in the discussion of the physical description of the material to which the conversion applies. The metric measurement may be noted in parentheses after the measurement in inches, as illustrated in some of the examples.

21 slides: col; 2 x 2 in. (5 x 5 cm.)

In printed catalogs limited to a specific medium, elements in the Collation which are common to all entries in the catalog may be omitted. For example, in a catalog listing 16mm sound films in color, the entry would omit medium designator, color statement, and size.

IX. SERIES (Area 6)

A series is a group of separate works, numbered or unnumbered, which are related to each other by content, and by the fact that each bears a collective title. Works in series are generally produced under the direction or sponsorship of one organization. The terms "series" and "set" are often used interchangeably in producers' catalogs.

A. Series

1. Series title. The series title is given in parentheses (*AACR*, 142A1) following the Collation, *in the form in which it appears on the work itself.*

1 reel: 10 min; sd; col; 16mm. (Consumer education)

If there are slight variations in the series title found on the individual items of the series, the most commonly used series title is selected for the series statement, and used in all series tracings (*AACR*, 142C). When main entry is under series title, the series statement is omitted unless the work(s) is part of another series or is a subseries.

Series titles should not be taken from the container (except when it is the primary source of information) or from vendors' and producers' catalogs. For promotional purposes, works may often be presented under new series titles or be regrouped into several different sets or series, and vendors' series titles may differ from those of the producer. A series title which is not shown on the work itself but appears prominently on its container may be given in a note if the work may be known or requested under that series title. An added entry may be made for it, if desired.

Series title on container: Old World civilizations.

If a series title is taken from a source other than the work itself and is recorded in the Series area, the source is given in a note.

Series title from container.

2. Numbering within the series. If the number on the work itself or a producer's catalog number indicates the sequence of the item in the series, the number should be included as part of the series title. Sequence numbering should not be supplied from other sources unless the sequential order is important for a specific purpose, such as when the use of items in sequence is necessary for content understanding where each item constitutes a progressive step in the development of the subject; or when the sequence number is necessary for filing when the main entry is under the series title and cards for the individual items are filed numerically rather than alphabetically within the series.

3. Works in more than one series. If a work is part of more than one series, all Series statements, each enclosed within its own set of parentheses, are given immediately following the Collation area (*AACR*, 142F1).

B. Subseries

If a major series contains a subseries, both the major series title and the subseries title should be given and an added entry made for each.

1 filmstrip: 43 fr; col; 35mm. (Basic English usage: Parts of speech; no. 3)

X. NOTES (Area 7)

Notes are designed to provide supplementary information about the nature and scope of the work, and any relationships not brought out in the formal description. They should be as brief as clarity and good grammar permit, and may be combined or grouped together to create a clear logical entry. The following types are generally useful, and should be given when applicable (*AACR*, 143-150).

A. Educational Level

The educational level for which the work is intended may be indicated following the Series notation. If a statement designating the intended audience level is not desired, it may be omitted. The following terms are used when appropriate, and may be abbreviated as shown:

For levels	*Use the term*	*Abbreviation*
Pre-school	Pre-school	K
Grades K-3	Primary	P
Grades 4-6	Intermediate	I
Grades 7-8	Junior high	J
Grades 9-12	Senior high	H
College and adult	Adult	A

If the work is suitable for a wide educational range, the span may be indicated by the use of two terms or abbreviations, e.g., K-I. Restrictions on the use or suitability of a work are given in a note.

For medical students only.
For Illinois residents only.

B. Extension of Physical Description

When special equipment is required, or when further specifications are desirable to describe the size or physical properties of the work, this information is noted.

For use with AutoTutor Mark 4.
Requires Cinemascope lens.
Slides synchronized with cassette.
Magnetic sound track.

C. Accompanying and/or Descriptive Material

Material accompanying the work which is designed to assist in its presentation or understanding is described in a note.

With teacher's guide.
With script.
With student guide.
With patient's guide and instructor's manual.
Program notes on container.

D. Other Versions.

Each version of a work in the collection in the same or a different medium is cataloged separately. Other versions that are known to exist may be given in a note.

Also issued in super 8mm.
Also issued in three separate consecutive films.
Also issued in French and Spanish.
Sound version (73 fr.) also issued.

E. Title

1. Source of title. Note the source of the title if it is not taken from the work itself.

Title from container.
Title from audio track of film.
Title from Chemical Abstracts Service specification manual.

2. Title variations. The original title, if known, and other titles under which the work is issued or has been previously released, with or without a change in content, are noted.

Originally released under the title Julie.
Also issued under the title Navaho: the last red Indians.
Released in England under the title Lord of plenty.

If the work is popularly known under a shortened or variant title, this title is noted, and an added entry is made for it.

Known also as The Blue boy.

F. Related Works

Other works upon which a work depends for its intellectual and artistic content are cited in a note. Author-title, author and/or title added entries are made for such works.

Adapted from a short story by O. Henry.
Based on Edwin Way Teale's book of the same title.
Based on the book Biological science: an inquiry into life, by the Biological Sciences Curriculum Study.

G. Credits

Credits may be given for individuals who have contributed to the creation of the work and whose names do not appear in the statement of creator responsibility: authors, editors, collaborators, content authorities, artists, cartographers, photographers, composers, conductors, musicians, producers, directors, actors, narrators, readers, lecturers, and commentators. The function or contribution is noted, followed by the person's name.

CREDITS: Producer, Mack Woodruff; directors, Marshall Franke, Jack Wellman.

Organizations which have made a contribution to the content may also be acknowledged.

The inclusion of these credits is optional, depending upon the requirements of the patrons served. If given, they are generally cited in the order in which they appear on the work itself. The caption "CREDITS" may be omitted.

New York Philharmonic Orchestra; conductor, Leonard Bernstein.

H. Summary

The Summary provides a brief, accurate, and objective statement of the subject content of the work sufficient to guide the potential user in selection. The caption "SUMMARY" may be omitted.

The content should be summarized in fifty words or less. Avoid repeating the title and subtitle, or any information adequately expressed by them. Omit adjectives, adverbs, and statements which do not contribute to an understanding of the content, e.g., "This film shows . . .", ". . . tells the story of . . .", etc. Always avoid promotional or evaluative phrases such as "an exciting film" or "an outstanding presentation". A succinct style is recommended, but clarity must not be sacrificed for brevity. Short phrases should be used when they will substitute adequately for complete sentences.

References to techniques used in the production (time lapse photography, slow motion photography, iconography, microphotography, animation, etc.) may be given when they are significant.

The Summary, together with the title and subtitle, should be sufficiently specific to guide the cataloger in the assignment of subject headings, and the user in the initial selection of appropriate material.

I. Contents

If a work consists of a number of parts, each of which has a distinctive title, these titles are given in a Contents note. The caption "CONTENTS", or "PARTIAL CONTENTS" may be omitted.

XI. OTHER IDENTIFYING AND ORGANIZATIONAL DATA (Area 8)

A. Standard Numbering (SN)

A ten digit identification number, similar in format to the International Standard Book Number (ISBN), is now being assigned to each version of every 16mm educational film.

The *Standard Number* consists of four units of information: 1) group identifier; 2) producer prefix; 3) unique title number; 4) check digit.

The *group identifier* "0" indicates that the principal office of the film's producer is in the United Kingdom, the United States of America, Eire, Australia or South Africa.

The *producer prefix* has from two to six digits, with the larger producers having the smaller numbers.

A unique *title number* is assigned to every variation of each title (long version, short version, black & white print, color print, revision, etc.).

The tenth digit is known as the *check digit*, and is mathematically calculated by a formula known as Modulus 11. The check digit almost precludes the possibility that any digit in the Standard Number could be inverted or transcribed incorrectly without being detected when the information is keyboarded into the computer.

Group Identifier	Producer Prefix	Title Number	Check Digit
0	- 01	-047523	- 0

The numbering of other nonbook formats may be considered at some future date. At that time, conforming to the position prescribed for the International Standard Book Number in the *International Standard Bibliographic Description (Monographs)*, the Standard Number might be included as the last element in the Notes area.

B. Tracings

To facilitate access to materials through the catalog or computer, appropriate subject headings and added entries should be assigned. The tracings, which are usually placed at the bottom of the card, constitute a record of the subject and added entries made for the work. This information is required so that all catalog cards may be withdrawn when the work is no longer in the collection. Tracings may also alert the user to subject headings under which additional material may be found.

1. Subject headings. Subject headings should be selected from approved subject heading lists such as *Library of Congress Subject Headings*, *Sears List of Subject Headings*, or other special subject indexes such as *MeSH*, the list of descriptors used in *Index Medicus*.

For consistency and systematic organization, the subject headings cited in these recommended sources should be carefully followed in the cataloging procedure. Considered departures from a standard listing may be necessary in developing indexes adapted to local needs and specialized collections. New and alternative terms used must be noted in the subject heading guide for future use. Each resource center should use the same subject heading list for its book and nonbook collections.

2. Added entries. In accordance with the *Anglo-American Cataloging Rules*, added entries should be made for those personal or corporate names, original or variant titles, and series titles under which a user might search for the work. Added entries for producer/publisher, sponsor, and distributor are not usually made.

The medium designator, enclosed in brackets and following the title, is included in an added entry which is for a work in an audiovisual medium other than the medium of the work being cataloged.

Folk songs of Latin America. [Audiorecording] Glendale, CA: Bowmar 145, c1966.
1 disc, 12 in: 16 min; 33.3 rpm. & 2 filmstrips entitled Latin American folk songs.

. . . .

. . . .

. . . .

FOLK SONGS, LATIN AMERICAN/ t: Latin American folk songs. [Filmstrip] (Tracings for added entries)

C. Classification Number

Classification numbers organize materials by subject and indicate their location. For organization by subject content, all formats of media should be classified by the same scheme. The use of the Library of Congress or Dewey Decimal classification schemes will achieve the subject integration of book and nonbook materials.

Subject classification permits both the integrated shelving of all types of materials, if desired, and an orderly arrangement in collections where specific media are stored separately. If classification is intended only as a locator, a simple sequential accession numbering system or the assignment of blocks of numbers to different types of media will suffice. Accessioning may be preferred for collections which are closed to the public, or require special shelving, security, or humidity control.

The bibliographic records for all books and audiovisuals should be filed together in the main catalog, even though some materials may be stored in separate areas.

D. Media Code

Automated procedures generally require that medium designators be coded. The same code should be used in manual systems if codification is desired.

1. General and specific designator code. Each medium may be coded either by the *general physical form designator (medium designator)* e.g., "FA" for Filmstrip, which includes both filmstrips and filmslips; or by the *specific physical form designator (specific designator)* which offers a separate coding "FL" for Filmslip and "FS" for Filmstrip, for those desiring to indicate the specific type of material. Even though not used, general and specific designator coding may be shown in the lower right corner of the shelf list and/or catalog card in anticipation of future need, e.g., "FA:FS", for Filmstrip.

The following coding is recommended:*

MEDIUM DESIGNATOR	SPECIFIC DESIGNATOR	CODE
Audiorecording		AA
	Cartridge	AR
	Cassette	AC
	Disc	AD
	Reel	AT
	Roll	AO
Archival/Experimental	Cylinder	AY
	Page	AS
	Wire	AW
Chart		CA
	Chart	CH
	Flannel board set	CL
	Flip chart	CF
	Graph	CG
	Magnetic board set	CM
	Relief chart	CR
	Wall chart	CW
Diorama		OA
	Diorama	OD
Filmstrip		FA
	Filmslip	FL
	Filmstrip	FS
Flash card		HA
	Card	HC
Game		GA
	Game	GM
	Puzzle	GP
	Simulation	GS

*A suggested listing of designators and coding for books and book-like materials and serials is contained in Appendix VII, p. 226.

MEDIUM DESIGNATOR	SPECIFIC DESIGNATOR	CODE
Globe		QA
	Globe	QG
	Relief globe	QR
Kit		KA
	Exhibit	KE
	Kit	KT
	Laboratory kit	KL
	Programed instruction kit	KP
Machine-readable data file		DA
Species of file	Data file	DF
	Program file	DE
Storage medium	Disc	DD
	Punched card	DB
	Punched paper tape	DP
	Tape	DT
Map		LA
	Map	LM
	Relief map	LR
	Wall map	LW
Microform		NA
	Aperture card	NC
	Card	ND
	Cartridge	NE
	Cassette	NF
	Fiche	NH
	Reel	NR
	Ultrafiche	NU
Model		EA
	Mock-up	EM
	Model	EE
Motion picture		MA
	Cartridge	MR
	Cassette	MC
	Loop	ML
	Reel	MP
Picture		PA
	Art original	PO
	Art print	PR
	Hologram	PH
	Photograph	PP
	Picture	PI
	Post card	PC
	Poster	PT
	Stereograph	PG
	Study print	PS

MEDIUM DESIGNATOR	SPECIFIC DESIGNATOR	CODE
Realia		RA
	Name of object	RO
	Specimen	RS
Slide		SA
	Audioslide	SO
	Microscope slide	SM
	Slide	SL
	Stereoscope slide	SS
Transparency		TA
	Transparency	TR
Videorecording		VA
	Cartridge	VR
	Cassette	VC
	Disc	VD
	Reel	VT

2. Media code and designators in the call number. When media materials are stored in separate areas, the general or specific medium coding or designator spelled out in full may be placed above the classification number to serve as a location device. The degree of specificity is determined by the media distinctions needed for shelving and retrieval. Coding is preferred above the classification number unless local demand for ease of recognition necessitates that the designator be spelled out in full.

3. Color code. The color coding of catalog cards to indicate that the material is in an audiovisual format or a specific medium is unwise. The number of media formats far exceeds the number of discernible colors available. The practice does not lend itself to computerized card production and generally increases the cost of cataloging.

Color coding is not recommended.

E. Additional Information

Some catalogs may require the inclusion of additional information such as purchase price, rental rate, regional or cooperative location, shelf number, Standard Account Number (SAN), etc. The position of this information in the catalog entry is not prescribed, but should be given in an appropriate area, e.g., purchase price and rental rate may be noted after the data in the Imprint area. For print materials price is given after the International Standard Book Number, or if there is no standard number, in the ISBN position (*AACR*, 149, footnote 25). In the same manner, price information for nonprint materials may be given following the Standard Number (see Basic Rule XI.A, p. 24), or if there is no standard number, in SN position.

SECTION TWO
CATALOGING OF SPECIFIC MEDIA

I. OVERVIEW

The basic rules for cataloging have been given in the preceding section. In this section their application is demonstrated. For works in each medium the information is presented in the same sequence as in Section I and references to the applicable basic rules are provided. The intent of the first statement which appears under Imprint (Area 4), Collation (Area 5), and Series (Area 6), is to show, for all formats, all the elements in each area as they would be recorded on the catalog card. For audiorecordings, filmstrips, and motion pictures, all areas are discussed in depth. *For works in other media, explanations are focused on those areas which contain details that are peculiar to the particular format or that are exceptions to the basic rules* (see p. 34 for details). The works cataloged on the sample cards were selected to show as comprehensively as possible how the basic rules can be applied and how problems can be handled. The examples can be used as a guide in the cataloging of similar materials and in the treatment of similar problems.

II. ARRANGEMENT OF ELEMENTS ON THE CATALOG CARD

The elements are recorded in area sequence as indicated in Section I: Arrangement of the Catalog Elements, p. 2.

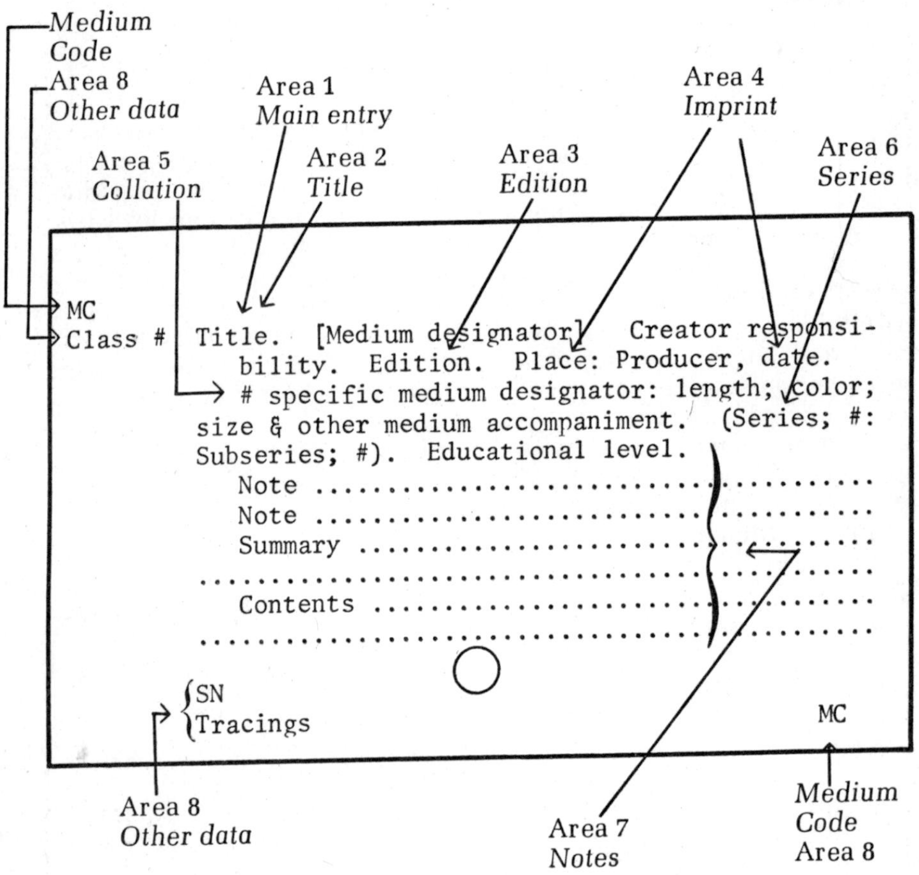

Figure 1. Arrangement of Elements: Title Main Entry.

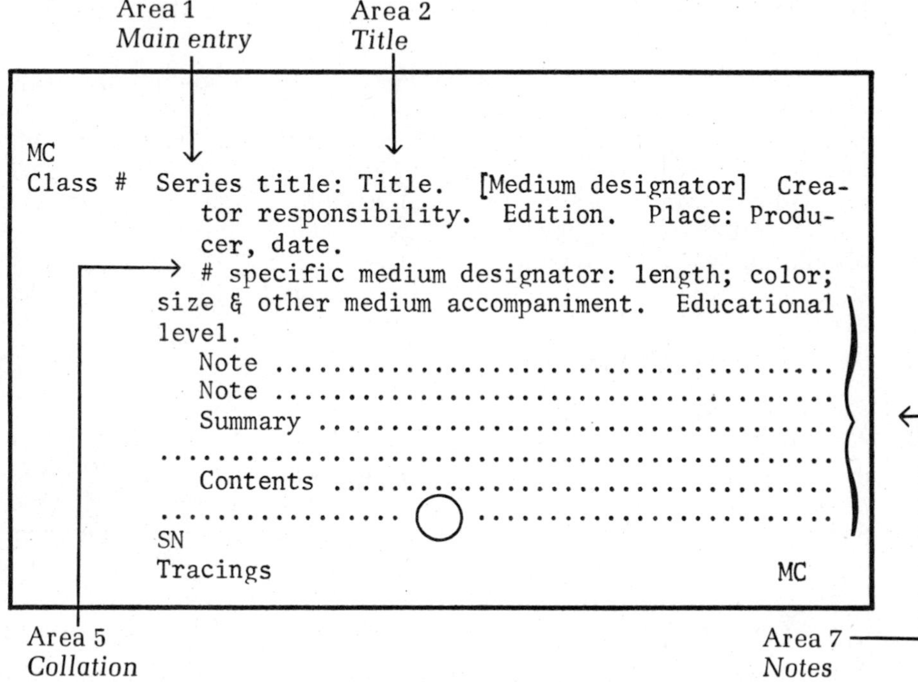

Figure 2. Arrangement of Elements: Series Title Main Entry. Area 6 (Series Title) is omitted.

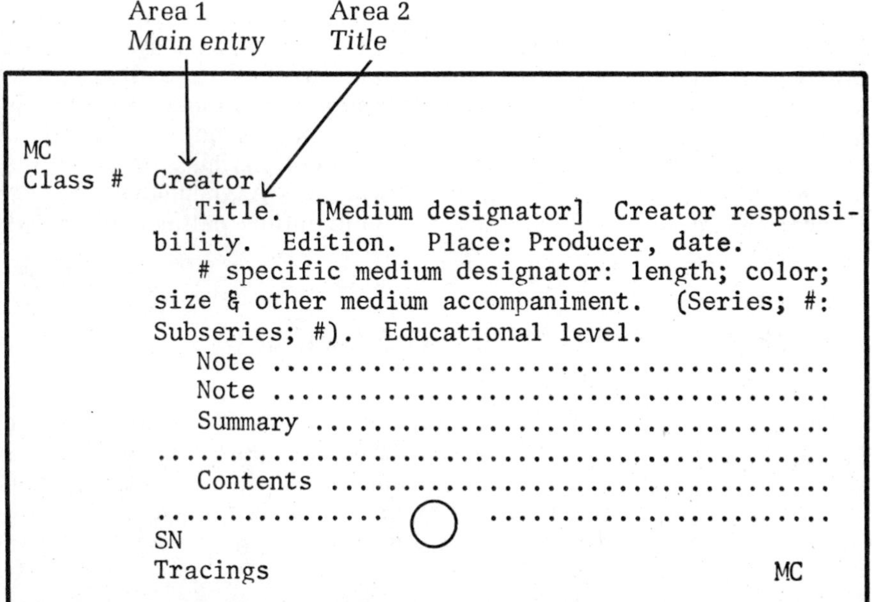

Figure 3. Arrangement of Elements: Creator Main Entry.

III. STYLE

The *Anglo-American Cataloging Rules* is the guide for abbreviations, capitalization, use of numerals, uniform titles, and other matters that pertain to style. As considered necessary, adaptations may be made to conform to current usage. For example, in film literature, the width of film is usually recorded as 8mm, 16mm, 35mm, omitting the space before the abbreviation "mm" and the period after it (see also Format of Cataloging Examples).

IV. PUNCTUATION

Chapter 6 (revised) of the *Anglo-American Cataloging Rules* details the punctuation prescribed by the *International Standard Bibliographic Description (Monographs)* for print materials. The basic pattern of punctuation, omitting specific punctuation peculiar to any one area, is:

> Areas are separated from each other by a period-space-dash-space (. --)
>
> Elements within an area are separated from each other by punctuation prescribed for the specific area (*AACR* 131 and punctuation rules for each area)
>
> In general, items within each element are separated from each other by a space-colon-space (:), a space-semicolon-space (;), a comma-space (,), or a period-space (.).

This basic punctuation pattern may also be followed in cataloging nonprint materials. ISBD(M) punctuation is primarily a system of signals which enables the eye or a machine to recognize, without understanding their content, the various elements that make up a bibliographic description. For those institutions that do not elect to follow the ISBD punctuation in every detail, adaptations may be made that accord with the standard punctuation practices in language usage. (See Format of Cataloging Examples for punctuation pattern on sample cards.)

V. FORMAT OF CATALOGING EXAMPLES

The primary intent of the card catalog examples is to show the content of the entry, not the typographical format. Each resource center will have developed a pattern of indentions, spacing, and arrangement of organizational elements for the catalog cards for print materials. This same pattern should be used for the catalog cards for nonprint materials.

Since printed catalog cards for all types of audiovisual materials are not yet widely available, the format of the sample cards used in this volume is designed for the typewritten card. The information is spaced to facilitate typing and maintain easy legibility. To minimize the number of continuation cards needed, the format, style, and punctuation presented in the *Anglo-American Cataloging Rules* have been modified in some respects.

1. Punctuation

a) The basic punctuation pattern is:

Areas are separated from each other by a period-space-space (.)

Elements within an area are separated from each other by a period-space-space (.)

Items within each element are separated from each other by a colon-space (:), a semicolon-space (;), a comma-space (,), or a period-space (.).

b) Periods are omitted after abbreviations if followed by another punctuation mark, e.g., (sd; 5 in:).

2. Tracings

a) Entries recorded in the tracings are separated by a slash mark-space (/).

b) Arrangement of entries. Subject headings are in capitals; followed by added entries in lower case, each arranged alphabetically; followed by title and series tracings.

c) Abbreviations. The following abbreviations are used in the tracings:

t	Title added entry
t: contents	Title added entry for all titles listed in the Contents note
ser	Series added entry.

VI. SUBJECT HEADINGS

The same subject heading list should be used for both print and nonprint materials. Subject headings on all sample cards are from *Sears List of Subject Headings*, 10th ed.

VII. CLASSIFICATION NUMBERS

In general, the same classification scheme should be used for both print and nonprint materials. For some storage facilities, however, an accession number system may be more practical. Except where an accession number is shown, classification numbers on all sample cards are from the *Abridged Dewey Decimal Classification*, 10th ed.

VIII. SPECIFIC MEDIA CATALOGING: RULES AND SAMPLE CARDS

The general principles for cataloging have been given in the preceding section. The application of these principles to each of the following type of medium is illustrated in the following section. In the application of the general rules to each medium, the appropriate basic rule in Section I is cited. The numbering and citation of basic rules is consistent with the numbering of the basic rules as given in Section I. If a rule has a unique application to a particular medium (e.g., the length of an audiorecording is measured differently than the length of a filmstrip), an explanation of that application of the rule is given. If no special application of a rule is required, the basic rule is cited without further explanation. If a basic rule does not apply at all, the reason for its non-applicability may be given.

The examples following the discussion of the rules are designed to show the content of the entry, not the typographical format.

Medium Designator: **AUDIORECORDING**

Specific Designators:
- Cartridge
- Cassette
- Disc
- Reel
- Roll
  - Archival/Experimental
    - Cylinder
    - Page
    - Wire

Description

An *audiorecording* is a registration of sound vibrations on a material substance by mechanical or electronic means so that sound may be reproduced. On a *disc* the sound is recorded in grooves cut in the revolving surface by a stylus responding to the sound vibrations. On a tape the sound is recorded magnetically on one surface which is coated with magnetic particles. A *cartridge* is a permanently encased single reel and tape which has the ends joined together to form a continuous loop that provides playback without rewinding. A *cassette* is a permanently encased tape that winds and rewinds from reel to reel. A *reel* is a tape mounted on an open reel. A *roll*, used in player-pianos, player-organs, or other similar mechanical instruments, is usually made of paper containing a pattern of holes that actuate the sound producing devices.

Specific Designators

Specific designators for some audio formats that are considered archival and experimental are listed as a separate group. Specific designators for such recordings may be formulated by the cataloger as needed. Before assigning a specific designator, however, the cataloger should ascertain that the recording is not already covered by an existing specific designator. For example, the recording in a music box may actually be a disc recording and should be designated as such, with a note describing the box which contains the recording. The same caution should be exercised in adopting specific designators for experimental formats (e.g., audiopage) or those advertised under a trade name as entirely new. The cataloger should also explore the possibility that the audio format described by the producer might not be cataloged as an audiorecording because it carries only the sound portion of a work in another medium. For example, an audioslide—a slide mounted in a magnetically coated frame or in one with a short length of audiotape on it—is cataloged as a slide, which is the dominant medium. An audiocard, which contains printed pictures or words and a strip of audiotape along the bottom edge, is cataloged as a flash card, which is the dominant medium.

When the specific designator is not used in context with the medium designator, "Audiorecording," (e.g., when audio material accompanies a work in a different medium) an ambiguity in medium may occur. In such cases, the combining form "audio" is added to the specific designator to identify its medium: audiocartridge, audiocassette, audiodisc, audioreel, audioroll.

MAIN ENTRY (Area 1)

In general, an audiorecording of a work originally produced in another medium is entered in the same manner as the original work. It should be emphasized, however, that the audiorecording is a new work which must be analyzed independently from the original. The transfer from a visual to an aural medium may involve additional significant intellectual and artistic contributions extensive enough to warrant a main entry different from that of the original work, for example, a musical composition in which improvisation is such that the audiorecording is considered an adaptation of the original composer's work and is entered under title or improvisor (see Creator Main Entry).

An audiorecording without a collective title which contains two or more works is entered under the creator or title, as appropriate, of the first work on side one of the recording (see Card 2). Separate or added entries are made for each of the other works (see Cards 2, 2A, 2B) depending upon the importance of the work and the clientele's need for a full description of the particular kind of work. For example, in a collection which is purposely music-oriented for its users, a separate entry would be made for each musical composition, but in a school media center collection, an added entry would suffice.

A. Title Main Entry. Apply Basic Rule IV.A, p. 4. Title main entry is preferred unless creator responsibility can be clearly attributed to a person or body *who is significant in identifying the audiorecording*. Main entry under title is also recommended for works in which music and words are so combined that the predominance of music or words is questionable. In such works, the creators of words and music are cited in the Statement of creator responsibility and added entries are made for them (see Card 3).

B. Series Title Main Entry. Each separate work that is included in a series or set is usually cataloged under its own title. In some instances, as discussed in Basic Rules IV.B1-3, it is advisable to use the series title for the main entry, and to consider the title of each individual recording as a subtitle of the series title.

C. Creator Main Entry. Apply Basic Rules IV.C1-3, p. 6. Musical and spoken audiorecordings which are substantially reproductions are usually entered under the composer or author of the original work.

Dramatizations, abridgments, and adaptations are entered under title (see Cards 2, 2A, 2B) unless the resource center wishes to keep together all versions of the works of each composer or author.

Recordings of collections or excerpts from collections are entered under title. The original compiler or editor of the collection is not regarded as the creator of the audiorecording since a different person is usually responsible for preparing the material for the sound production. The original compiler or editor may be cited in the Statement of creator responsibility or in a note, and an added entry may be made for his name.

An audiorecording may be entered under the name of a performer or performing group when the artistic interpretation of a work is considered of prime importance and the name is significant in identifying the work (see Cards 5, 6, 11A). Entry under performer may frequently occur in recordings of popular music and in improvisations since the requestor usually identifies them by performer and expects to find the renditions of each performer kept together.

TITLE/MEDIUM DESIGNATOR/STATEMENT OF CREATOR RESPONSIBILITY (Area 2)

A. Title. Apply Basic Rules V.A1-10, p. 7. The title is taken from the label on the audiorecording (disc, roll), on the mount (reel), or on the case (cartridge, cassette) in which it is permanently enclosed. In some instances the title may be given only orally in the recording itself. If the label or recording does not provide sufficient information, the title is taken from the container (slipcase, album), accompanying notes, producer's catalog, or other reliable reference source. When label and container titles differ, the title on the container may be preferred if it identifies and describes the work more adequately. The source of title is given in a note, as are other significant title variations, and added entries may be made for variant titles by which the work may be known. If no title is found, one may be supplied by the cataloger and shown in brackets.

When an audiorecording contains two or more works, the titles of all the works are included in the title statement if they are equally prominent on the label (see Card 2). However, if such a listing results in a very lengthy title statement, the title of the first work only is cited in title position, and the titles of the other works are given in the Contents note. When any of the works is cataloged as a separate entry, its title is omitted from the title statement and is cited in a "With" note (see Notes, Content and Cards 2A, 2B).

A uniform title may be required, especially for muscial compositions, to bring together the entries for all the versions, arrangements, and titles by which a work is known. The uniform title consists essentially of the title under which the work was originally issued, or alternatively, the title by which the work is most commonly cited in the literature. Chapter 4 and rules 233-243 of the *Anglo-American Cataloging Rules* should be consulted for guidance in the formulation and use of uniform titles for non-musical and musical works. The uniform title, enclosed in square brackets, is noted on the first line of the body of the entry, between the main entry heading and the title of the audiorecording (see Cards 4, 9, 9A). When a uniform title is used for main entry, or is indicated in the tracings, the brackets are omitted.

B. Medium Designator. Apply Basic Rule V.B1, p. 10. The general physical form designator (medium designator), "Audiorecording," is given in the singular form following the Title statement and is usually enclosed in brackets. The brackets may be omitted (see Card 9B).

When a uniform title is required, the medium designator follows the uniform title instead of the title of the audiorecording.

C. Statement of Creator Responsibility. Apply Basic Rule V.C, p. 13. The function(s) performed and the name(s) of creators such as editors, compilers, performers, directors, and producers may be cited *if they are significant in identifying the work.*

EDITION (Area 3)

Apply Basic Rule VI, p. 14. A reissue of an old recording, even though produced by another company, is not regarded as a new edition. Information which identifies the original recording, such as title, producer, serial number, and date, is given in a note (see Other Versions and Card 6).

IMPRINT (Area 4)*

Place: Producer, producer's serial identification, copyright/production date; sponsored by Sponsor; Place: Distributed/Released by Distributor, release date.

A. Place. Apply Basic Rule VII.A, p. 15. Frequent changes in the existence, organization, names, and locations of recording companies often make it difficult to ascertain where the producer's business office is located. When the information is not readily available place may be omitted; or the notation "[s.l.]" may be used to indicate that location is unknown.

*The first statement under Imprint, Collation, and Series, shows all the elements in each area as they would be recorded on the catalog card.

B. Producer/Sponsor/Distributor. Apply Basic Rules VII.B1-4, p. 16.

Serial identification. Because one or several producers may issue recordings of various performances of the same work, and titles are often very similar, an audiorecording requires a more exact identification than that provided by the title. For this purpose, the producer's serial number which appears on the recording and/or on the album or set is noted after the name of the producer. The matrix number, which is the number assigned to the master from which the recording is produced, is used only when the serial identification is lacking. The serial number is transcribed as it appears on the work. For consecutive numbers, the first and last are given, separated by a dash. For nonconsecutive, all the numbers are noted, separated by commas. For albums or sets, the number assigned to the entire set is recorded, followed parenthetically by the numbers of the individual recordings if they are different than the serial number of the set.

RCA Victor LSP 4366, c1971.
Vanguard VSD 5-6, [1970] (Consecutive)
Angel Records 36001, 36004, [1970] (Non-consecutive)
Columbia D2S 779 (DS 7126-7127) c1968. (Album, individual recordings)
Capitol SP 8673, SPAO 8694, [1968- (Open entry)
T&T Records matrix no. T-74354, 1969.

C. Date. Apply Basic Rule VII.C, p. 17. On audiorecordings the copyright date is preceded by the symbol "℗". In cataloging, the date is preceded by the letter "c"* which is used to denote copyright for all other types of materials. The copyright/production date is recorded following the producer's serial identification. When a copyright/production date is lacking, a date of release, if known, is given. If neither the copyright, production, or release date can be established, a probable date is shown in brackets. The abbreviation "n.d." signifying "no date" should not be used.

COLLATION (PHYSICAL DESCRIPTION) (Area 5)

Number of cartridge(s)/cassette(s)/disc(s)/reel(s)/roll(s), diameter of disc(s)/reel(s): number of minutes; inches per second/revolutions per minute; monophonic/stereophonic/quadraphonic & accompaniments; other physical characteristics.

*For audiorecordings, the interim revision of Chapter 14 of the AACR uses "p" preceding the copyright date.

A. Number of Items and Specific Designator

2 cartridges: 6 cassettes: 3 discs, 12 in. (30 cm.):
1 reel, 5 in. (13 cm.): 1 roll:

Give the diameter of discs and reels following the specific designator. Metric measurement is preferred, but until the conversion is well understood, the diameter may be shown in inches, followed, if desired, by the centimeter measurement in parentheses. The metric measurements for disc and reel diameters are:

3 in. ..... 8 cm. 5 in. ..... 13 cm. 7 in. ..... 18 cm.
10 in. ..... 25 cm. 12 in. ..... 30 cm.

If the diameter of the reel is not considered important for playback or storage purposes, it may be omitted. The dimensions of cassettes and cartridges are given following the specific designator only if they are other than the standard size of 3⅞ × 2½ in. (10 × 6.5 cm.) for cassettes or 5¼ × 7⅞ in. (13 × 20 cm.) for cartridges.

For rolls, the Collation statement includes only the number of items and the specific designator. No physical details are given.

C. Length. If readily available, give the total time duration in minutes using the abbreviation "min." When different works are recorded on each side of a recording the duration of each side may be given (e.g. 25, 30 min. a side, 30 min. each side) or the time may be omitted from the Collation and recorded after each title in the Contents note. When the entry includes more than one recording, give the total time of all the recordings or the span of time, such as 25-45 min., or omit the time from the Collation and record it after each title in the Contents note. Alternatively, time notation may be omitted entirely, especially when the recording contains several selections which are each of a relatively short duration. When durations appear on the labels or container, this information may be given in a note (see Extension of Physical Description).

F. Size. The width of reel tape is given only if it is other than ¼ inch (e.g., 1½ in.).

G. Playback speed. Give the playing speed of discs in revolutions per minute, abbreviated to "rpm." (16, 33.3, 45, 78 rpm.); of tapes (cartridge, cassette, reel) in inches (or centimeters) per second, abbreviated to "ips" (or cmps). The metric conversions for tape speeds are:

1⅞ ips. .... 4.75 cm. per second
3.75 ips. .... 9.5 cm. per second
7.5 ips. .... 19 cm. per second

For standard cassettes, which all play at 1⅞ ips., the speed may be omitted. For non-standard cassettes (e.g., "Unisette") the playback speed must be given. Playing speed is not given for rolls.

H. Recording mode. Indicate whether the recording is monophonic, stereophonic, or quadraphonic, using the abbreviations "mono.", "stereo.", or "quad." "Mono." may be omitted since monophonic recordings may be played on all types of equipment.

I. Accompaniments. Works in a visual medium, such as filmstrips, slides, etc., which are issued with an audiorecording to convey its concepts more completely are considered dependent works or integral accompaniments. Their description, preceded by "&", is given after the recording mode. The information includes the number of items, the specific designator, the physical description, and other pertinent identifying facts which can be stated succinctly. The physical details are stated as prescribed in the Collation for the particular type of material (see Card 15). These may be omitted (see Card 15A) except when they indicate the necessity for a special kind of projection equipment.

With physical details of dependent work:
2 cassettes: 30 min. each; stereo. & 2 filmstrips: 60 fr. each; col; 35mm.

Without physical details of dependent work:
2 cassettes: 30 min. each; stereo. & 2 filmstrips.

J. Other Physical Characteristics. Note other physical characteristics which may be pertinent to the utilization or storage of the audiorecording, such as the width of the groove for discs, the number of tracks for tapes, the number and description of the containers. Discs of 33.3 and 45 rpm. are cut in microgroove. Discs of 78 rpm. are cut in standard groove. Sleeves, slipcases, albums, boxes, cassette binders, and other types of audiorecording packaging are all called "containers". Dimensions are not usually given except for casette or cartridge containers designed for storage on standard library shelving.

Microgroove.
Standard groove.
4-track.
8-track.
In 3 containers.
In container, 21 × 13 cm.

SERIES (Area 6)

(Series title; number within the series: Subseries title; number within the subseries).

Apply Basic Rules IX.A,B, p. 20.

NOTES (Area 7)

Apply Basic Rules X.A-I, p. 21. Notes are designed to provide supplementary information about the audiorecording not brought out in the formal description. They should be as brief as clarity and good grammar permit, and may be combined or grouped together to create a clear informational and descriptive statement. The fullness of detail will vary according to the needs of the particular clientele.

A. Educational Level. If desired, the educational level for which the audiorecording is intended may be noted following the Series statement. The terms or abbreviations given in Basic Rule X.A, p. 21, are used. Or, the educational level, audience suitability, and/or restrictions may be described in the Summary.

B. Extension of Physical Description. Give any additional information required for a more complete description of the physical properties of the audiorecording and of special equipment needed.

Manual sequence.
Automatic sequence.
Audible advance signals.
Various durations.
Durations listed on labels.
Durations on container.
For player piano.
Music box disc.

C. Accompanying and/or Descriptive Material. Describe material designed to assist in the understanding of the audiorecording(s).

Program notes on container.
Biographical notes on container; text, with English translation, 10 p., inserted.
Teacher's guide bound in container.

Significant information which may be derived from accompanying and/or descriptive material or from other sources may be given as a separate note or combined with other notes. The form of the work (e.g., poems, drama, songs, operetta) is indicated if it is not evident from the title. Place and date of performance, recording history, language of the text, etc., may also be noted.

Principally songs.
Songs with instrumental accompaniment.
Opera in English.
Cantata.
Short stories.
Tragedy in 4 acts.
Motion picture sound track.
Recorded live at the Coliseum, Oakland, CA, Apr. 26, 1972.

D. Other Versions. Each version of an audiorecording in the collection is cataloged separately. To minimize repetitive cataloging, the various versions in the collection may be listed on one card. Give sufficient information to identify differences in physical characteristics and location (see Card 12).

Other versions that are not in the collection and are known to exist may be noted.

Also issued in cassette.
Also issued as a set of 4 discs.

When the work is a reissue of an old audiorecording, give any information which identifies the original recording, such as title, producer, serial number, and date.

Previously issued under serial no. 17643.
A reissue of Columbia C-68, 1948.

E1. Source of Title. Note the source of the title if it is not taken from the labels or the audio track of the recording.

Title from container.
Title from accompanying notes.

E2. Title Variations. Title variations frequently occur in audiorecordings. There may be differences in the title which appears on the label, on the container, in the accompanying notes, and in the producer's catalog. These titles and their sources are noted if they are significant in identifying the recording.

Modern rhythm band tunes. (Main entry title from label)
With teacher's guide entitled Modern rhythm band music. (Accompanying and/or descriptive material note)
Title on container: Modern tunes for rhythms and instruments. (Title variation note)

Negro folk rhythms. (Main entry title from label)
Title on container: American Negro folk and work song rhythms. (Title variation note)
Also known as Negro work songs. (Title variation note)

F. Related Works. Cite works upon which the audiorecording depends for its intellectual and/or artistic content.

A dramatization from the book by Armstrong Sperry.
Songs from the sound track of the motion picture Deliverance.
Coordinates with the book of the same title compiled by Carl Parrish and John F. Ohl.
Improvisations on the theme from Fiddler on the roof.

G. Credits. Give the names of performers and performing groups whose contributions are significant in creating the work and whose names have not been cited elsewhere. The type of performance, the instrument(s) played, or the function performed is noted, followed by the performer's name. The function and names of conductors, directors, featured singers, leading actors, or other persons creatively associated with a performing group (e.g., orchestra, chorus, instrumental ensemble, theater company) are stated after the name of the group. Added entries may be made as considered necessary. The caption "CREDITS" is generally not used for the performer note, and names may be combined with information in other notes.

Read by Boris Karloff.
Narrator, Edward R. Murrow.
San Francisco Symphony Orchestra; conductor, Seiji Ozawa.
Flute, Hubert Barwahser; Concertgebouw Orchestra; conductor, Willem van Otterloo.

When the recording contains several works, each performed by a different person or group, the listing of names may become too long to be practical. In such cases, names may be omitted and the term "various" may be used to indicate that the work is performed by several different people.

Various Danish soloists and ensembles; directed by Mogens Wöldike.
Various readers.

H. Summary. Provide a brief statement of the subject content of the work. The supplementary information given in other notes may be combined in the Summary statement. The caption "SUMMARY" may be omitted.

I. Contents. When an audiorecording contains several works their titles are listed in the Contents note. Creators and performers for each different work may also be identified. If the selections are so numerous that a complete listing is impractical, a partial listing may suffice; or the titles on specified bands or sides of the recording may be indicated; or the Contents note may be omitted in favor of an informal listing included in the Summary statement. The captions "CONTENTS" or "PARTIAL CONTENTS" may be omitted.

"With" note. A "With" note follows or replaces the Contents note* when separate entries are made for different works contained in an audiorecording. The works are listed in the order indicated on the label, and the information is recorded in the sequence and form in which it appears in the separate entry. If the work requires a uniform title, the uniform title, not the label title, is given in the "With" note.

---

*The "With" note may precede the Extension of physical description note (see interim revision of Chapter 14, AACR).

OTHER IDENTIFYING AND ORGANIZATIONAL DATA (Area 8)

Apply Basic Rules XI.A-E, p. 24.

B2. Added entries. In addition to the added entries usually made for names and titles, added entries should be made for performers and performing groups under which a user might search for the work. When a work requires a uniform title, the uniform title is used in the added entry. A proliferation of added entries for these works can be avoided by using *see* and *title references* (see Cards 13, 14, 14A). Title added entries are not made for non-distinctive label or uniform titles, such as those which indicate the type or form of the work, e.g., Symphony no. 5; Sonata, piano, no. 21.

D. Media Code. All audiorecordings may be coded under the general designator coding for audiorecordings "AA", or each format may be coded separately under the coding for its specific designator.

Cartridge	AR
Cassette	AC
Disc	AD
Reel	AT
Roll	AO

The following specific designators and coding are suggested for archival and experimental formats:

Cylinder	AY
Page	AS
Wire	AW

Cataloging of Musical Works. The following examples do not show extensive detail for musical works. The cataloger should consult Chapter 13 of the *Anglo-American Cataloging Rules* if full descriptive cataloging consistent with that used for music is required.

AA
784.6 Children's songs. [Audiorecording] New York:
CHI Folkways Records FC 7036, c1964.
1 disc, 10 in: 33.3 rpm. K-P.
Lyric sheet in container.
Fourteen songs sung by Johnny Richardson
accompanying himself on the guitar.

CHILDREN'S SONGS/ Richardson, John

CARD 1
Audiorecording, disc.
Title main entry.
General medium code in call number.
Educational level note.

956.1 The Fall of Constantinople. Lawrence of Arabia.
FAL [Audiorecording] Script by Elise Bell. New
York: Enrichment Materials EWR 313, c1970.
1 disc, 12 in: 33.3 rpm. (World landmark
series) J-H.
Notes in container.
Dramatizations with music and sound effects,
from the books by Bernardine Kielty, and Alis-
tair MacLean.
ISTAMBUL- SIEGE, 1453/ LAWRENCE, THOMAS/ Bell,
Elise/ Kielty, Bernardine/ MacLean, Alistair/
t: Lawrence of Arabia,/ ser

CARD 2
Audiorecording, disc: 2 works without collective title.
Main entry under title of 1st work.
2d work in title statement.
Statement of creator responsibility.
Series note.
Added entries for 2d work.

```
956.1   The Fall of Constantinople.  [Audiorecording]
FAL        Script by Elise Bell.  New York: Enrichment
           Materials EWR 313, c1970.
           1 disc, 12 in: 33.3 rpm.  (World landmark
        series)  J-H.
           Notes in container.
           A dramatization with music and sound effects,
        from the book by Bernardine Kielty.
           With: Lawrence of Arabia.
        ISTAMBUL- SIEGE, 1453/ Bell, Elise/ Kielty,
        Bernardine/ ser
```

CARD 2A
Audiorecording, disc: 2 works without collective title.
Separate entries for each work (1st work).
"With" note.

```
956.1   Lawrence of Arabia.  [Audiorecording]  Script
LAW        by Elise Bell.  New York: Enrichment Materi-
           als EWR 313, c1970.
           1 disc, 12 in: 33.3 rpm.  (World landmark
        series)  J-H.
           Notes in container.
           A dramatization with music and sound effects,
        from the book by Alistair MacLean.
           With: The Fall of Constantinople.
        LAWRENCE, THOMAS/ Bell, Elise/ MacLean, Alis-
        tair/ ser
```

CARD 2B
Audiorecording, disc: 2 works without collective title.
Separate entries for each work (2d work).
"With" note.

AD
782.8 Man of La Mancha; original motion picture sound-
MAN track. [Audiorecording] Lyrics by Joe
Darion. Music by Mitch Leigh, adapted & conducted by Laurence Rosenthal. Hollywood, CA: United Artists Records UAS 9906, [1972]
1 disc, 12 in: 33.3 rpm; stereo.
Durations listed on labels.
Starring Peter O'Toole, Sophia Loren, and James Coco.
MOVING PICTURE MUSIC- EXCERPTS/ MUSICAL REVUES, COMEDIES, ETC.- EXCERPTS/ Darion, Joseph/ Leigh, Mitch/ Rosenthal, Laurence

CARD 3
Audiorecording, disc: motion picture sound track.
Title main entry (same as motion picture).
Specific medium code in call number.
Added entries may be made for actors cited.

786.1 Mozart, Johann Chrysostom Wolfgang Amadeus
MOZ [Trios, piano & strings] [Audiorecording]
The six piano trios. Musical Heritage Society MHS 1340-1342, [1972]
3 discs, 12 in: 33.3 rpm; stereo.
Manual sequence.
Program notes by Gottfried Kraus and Hans Schurich in container.
Salzburg Mozart Trio performing on 18th century instruments.
PIANO TRIOS- TO 1800/ Mozart Trio of Salzburg/ t: The six piano trios.

CARD 4
Audiorecording, disc set.
Creator (composer) main entry.
Uniform title.
Place omitted.

```
784.8   Blood, Sweat, and Tears (Musical group)
BLO        New blood.  [Audiorecording]  New York: Colum-
        bia KC 31780, [1972]
           1 disc, 12 in: 33.3 rpm; stereo.
           Durations listed on labels.
           Song lyrics, 2 p., in container.
           CONTENTS: Down in the flood.- Touch me.-
        Alone.- Velvet.- I can't move no mountains.-
        Over the hill.- So long Dixie.- Snow queen.-
        Maiden voyage.
        MUSIC, POPULAR (SONGS, ETC.)- U.S./ t
```

CARD 5
Audiorecording, disc.
Creator (performing group) main entry.
Contents note.

```
784.8   Holiday, Billie
HOL        Strange fruit.  [Audiorecording]  New York:
        Atlantic SD 1614, [1972]
           1 disc, 12 in: 33.3 rpm.
           Durations and notes by L. Feather on container.
           Reissue of recordings made in 1939 and 1944.
           Sixteen popular songs of former years, sung
        by Billie Holiday with orchestral accompaniment.


        MUSIC, POPULAR (SONGS, ETC.)- U.S./ t
```

CARD 6
Audiorecording, disc.
Creator (performer) main entry.
Other versions note.

```
792.2   Golden age of comedy.  [Audiorecording]  New York:
GOL        Evolution 3013
           [1972-
               discs, 12 in: 33.3 rpm; stereo.
           Durations listed on labels.
           Program notes on containers.
           Performances by various comedians.


        AMERICAN WIT AND HUMOR/ COMEDY
```

CARD 7
Audiorecording, disc: open entry.
Title main entry.

```
812     O'Neill, Eugene Gladstone
ONE        Long day's journey into night.  [Audiorecord-
        ing]  Boston: Caedmon TRS 350, [1972?]
           4 discs, 12 in: 33.3 rpm; stereo.
           Durations listed on labels; automatic sequence.
           Program notes by L. Sheaffer on container.
           Play; Robert Ryan, Stacy Keach, Geraldine
        Fitzgerald, with James Naughton and Paddy Croft;
        director, Arvin Brown.

        Fitzgerald, Geraldine/ Keach, Stacy/ Ryan,
        Robert/ t
```

CARD 8
Audiorecording, disc set.
Creator (author) main entry.
Added entries may be made for other actors and director.

```
785.1   Beethoven, Ludwig van
BEE        [Symphony no. 9, op. 125, D minor]  [Audio-
        recording]
           Symphony no. 9 in D minor, op. 125 (Choral).
        New York: RCA R8S 1296, c1972.
           1 cartridge: 68 min; 3.75 ips; stereo; 8-track.
           With program notes and choral text with
        English translation.
           Disc and cassette also issued.
           Title on container: The world's favorite
        symphonies.

                                        (See next card)
```

CARD 9
Audiorecording, cartridge.
Creator (composer) main entry.
Uniform title.
Various notes.

```
                                                 (Card 2)

785.1   Beethoven, Ludwig van
BEE        [Symphony no. 9, op. 125, D minor]  [Audio-
        recording]
           Symphony no. 9 in D minor, op. 125 (Choral).
        RCA R8S 1296, c1972.

           Chicago Symphony Orchestra and Chorus; conduc-
        tor, Fritz Reiner; soprano, Phyllis Curtin; con-
        tralto, Florence Kopleff; tenor, John McCollum;
        bass, Donald Gramm.
        SYMPHONIES/ Chicago Symphony Orchestra/ Reiner,
        Fritz/ t: The            world's favorite
        symphonies.
                                                 AA:AR
```

CARD 9A
Continuation card.
Added entries may be made for vocalists cited.
Medium code at bottom of card.

785.1 Beethoven, Ludwig van
BEE Symphony no. 9 in D minor, op. 125 (Choral). Audiorecording. RCA R8S 1296, c1972.
1 cartridge: 68 min; 3.75 ips; stereo; 8-track.
With notes.
Chicago Symphony Orchestra and Chorus; conductor, Fritz Reiner; various vocal soloists.

SYMPHONIES/ Reiner, Fritz

CARD 9B
Audiorecording, cartridge.
Simplified cataloging.
Medium designator without brackets.

810.8 America's golden age. [Audiorecording] New
AME Rochelle, NY: Spoken Arts Mini-kit 17, 1971.
6 cassettes.
Various readers.
CONTENTS: The great stone face, by N. Hawthorne.- The minister's black veil, by N. Hawthorne.- Ralph Waldo Emerson: Poems and essays.- Walden, by Thoreau.- Henry Wadsworth Longfellow.- Anthology of 19th century American poets.

AMERICAN LITERATURE- COLLECTIONS/ t: contents

CARD 10
Audiorecording, cassette set.
Set title main entry.
Contents note.
Release date.

```
786.2   Keyboard immortal Josef Lhevinne plays again,
KEY        in stereo.  [Audiorecording]  Sun Valley, CA:
           Superscope  3-A071-S, c1970.
           1 reel, 7 in. (18 cm.): 3.75 ips; stereo.
        (The Keyboard immortal series; no. 8)
           Program notes and durations on container.
           Recorded by the Welte reproducing piano from
        piano rolls.
           Contains sonatas, etudes, nocturnes, and pre-
        ludes by Beethoven, Weber, Chopin, Dohnanyi,
        and Rachmaninoff.
        PIANO MUSIC/              Lhevinne, Josef/ ser
```

CARD 11
Audiorecording, reel.
Title main entry.
Metric conversion of reel size.

```
782.6   Lhevinne, Josef
LHE        Keyboard immortal Josef Lhevinne plays again,
        in stereo.  [Audiorecording]  Sun Valley, CA:
        Superscope 3-A071-S, c1970.
           1 reel, 7 in. (18 cm.): 3.75 ips; stereo.
        (The Keyboard immortal series; no. 8)
           Program notes and durations on container.
           Recorded by the Welte reproducing piano from
        piano rolls.
           Contains sonatas, etudes, nocturnes, and pre-
        ludes by Beethoven, Weber, Chopin, Dohnanyi, and
        Rachmaninoff.
        PIANO MUSIC/ t/          ser
```

CARD 11A
Audiorecording, reel.
Creator (performer) main entry.

783.6 Pops goes Christmas. [Audiorecording] New York:
POP RCA Red Seal, [1972]
Versions in collection:
AD 1 disc, 12 in: 33.3 rpm; stereo. LSC 3324.
AR 1 cartridge: 3.75 ips; stereo; 8-track. R8S 1304.
AC 1 cassette: stereo. RK 1304.
Durations and notes on containers.
Arthur Fiedler conducting his orchestra, his chorus, and the Boston Pops Orchestra perform Christmas carols, popular songs, and instrumental music.
CHRISTMAS- SONGS AND MUSIC/ Boston Pops Orchestra/ Fiedler, Arthur

CARD 12
Audiorecording: one entry for all formats in collection.
Title main entry.
Specific medium code for each format.

Stravinskiĭ, Igor' Fedorovich
The rite of spring

See

Stravinskiĭ, Igor' Fedorovich
Le sacre du printemps.

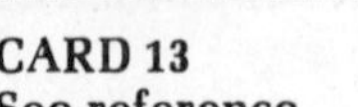

CARD 13
See reference.

The rite of spring
Stravinskiĭ, Igor' Fedorovich

Editions of this work will be found under

Stravinskiĭ, Igor' Fedorovich
Le sacre du printemps.

CARD 14
Title reference.

Le sacre du printemps
Stravinskiĭ, Igor' Fedorovich

Editions of this work will be found under the composer's name.

CARD 14A
Title reference.

784.7 Folk songs of Africa. [Audiorecording] Edited
FOL by Roberta McLaughlin. Glendale, CA: Bowmar
154, c1965.
1 disc, 12 in: 26 min; 33.3 rpm. & 2 filmstrips: 44, 35 fr; col; 35mm.
With lyric guide.
SUMMARY: Filmstrips provide words, notation,
and pictures descriptive of the Central African
culture each song represents.
AFRICA, CENTRAL- SOCIAL LIFE AND CUSTOMS/ FOLK
SONGS, AFRICAN/ McLaughlin, Roberta

CARD 15
Audiorecording, disc: with work in another medium.
Title main entry.

784.7 Folk songs of Africa. Audiorecording. Bowmar
FOL 154, c1965.
1 disc, 12 in: 26 min; 33.3 rpm. & 2 filmstrips.
With lyric guide.
Songs from Central Africa, illustrated by the
filmstrips.

AFRICA, CENTRAL- SOCIAL LIFE AND CUSTOMS/ FOLK
SONGS, AFRICAN

CARD 15A
Audiorecording, disc: with work in another medium.
Title main entry.
Simplified cataloging.

Medium Designator: **CHART**

Specific Designators:
- Chart
- Flannel board set
- Flip chart
- Graph
- Magnetic board set
- Relief chart
- Wall chart

Description

A *chart* is an opaque sheet exhibiting information in graphic or tabular form, or by the use of contours, shapes, or precut figures. *Flip charts* are a set of subject integrated charts hinged at the top which can be flipped in a progressive presentation. A *flannel board* is a display board covered with flannel or a comparable cloth to which pictured symbols backed with the same or a similar material (e.g., sandpaper) adhere. For cataloging purposes, felt boards, hook and loop boards, and other boards covered with fabric are included in the term "flannel board". A flannel board in itself is usually regarded as equipment and is not cataloged as a chart. A *flannel board set* contains the symbols that form a chart when they are displayed. The set may or may not include the flannel board. A *magnetic board* is a sheet of metal to which objects may be attached by means of magnets. When coated with chalkboard paint it may also be used as a chalkboard and is often called a magnetic chalkboard. A magnetic board in itself is usually regarded as equipment and is not cataloged as a chart. A *magnetic board set* contains the magnetized objects that make a chart when they are placed on the board. The set may or may not include the magnetic board. A *relief chart* presents graphic information in a raised or three-dimensional form.

Charts are issued singly and in sets. Those that are of temporary value because of poor durability or continuously changing data should be treated as vertical file material.

MAIN ENTRY (Area 1)

Apply Basic Rules IV.A-C, p. 4.

A. Title Main Entry. Title main entry is preferred for charts since they are usually identified by title by the producer and the user.

B. Series Title Main Entry. When charts are issued in sets they are usually entered under the title of the set or series. When an individual chart in the set is cataloged as a separate entity, its title is treated as a subtitle of the set title (see Card 18).

C. Creator Main Entry. A chart may be entered under the name of an individual if it is determined that the person is principally responsible for the conception and design, and if the name appears on the chart itself and *is significant in its identification* (see Card 18). Charts should not be entered under the name of a commercial producer.

TITLE/MEDIUM DESIGNATOR/STATEMENT OF CREATOR RESPONSIBILITY (Area 2)

A. Title. Apply Basic Rules V.A1-10, p. 7. The title is taken from the face of the chart. If the titles vary, preference is given to the most conspicuous title or to the title in the lower margin. If no title is found, a title may be taken from accompanying material such as a teacher's guide, or from the producer's catalog; or a title that indicates the subject of the chart may be supplied by the cataloger and enclosed in brackets.

B. Medium Designator. Apply Basic Rule V.B1, p. 10. The general physical form designator (medium designator) "Chart" is given in the singular form following the Title statement and is usually enclosed in square brackets. The brackets may be omitted.

C. Statement of Creator Responsibility. Apply Basic Rule V.C, p. 13.

EDITION (Area 3)

Apply Basic Rule VI, p. 14.

IMPRINT (Area 4)*

Place: Producer, copyright/production date; sponsored by Sponsor; Place: Distributed/Released by Distributor, release date.

Apply Basic Rules VII.A-C, p. 15.

COLLATION (PHYSICAL DESCRIPTION) (Area 5)

Number of chart(s)/flannel board set(s)/flip charts/graph(s)/magnetic board set(s)/relief chart(s)/wall chart(s); color/black and white; height × width in centimeters; mount, etc.

*The first statement under Imprint, Collation, and Series, shows all the elements in each area as they would be recorded on the catalog card.

A. Number of Items and Specific Designator

1 chart: 1 flannel board set: 20 flip charts:
5 graphs: 1 magnetic board set: 1 relief chart:
3 wall charts:

In simplified cataloging, if the entry describes only one chart, the number and the specific designator "chart" may be omitted since it is the same as the general designator.

When a chart qualifies for more than one specific designator, e.g., a relief chart that is also a wall chart, the specific designator should be selected that describes the physical characteristic judged to be the most meaningful for concept content. The other physical characteristic is described in a note (see Card 19).

E. Color Statement. The abbreviation "col." is used for color charts, "b&w" for black and white charts.

F. Size. Give the height times the width in centimeters, using the abbreviation "cm."

J. Other Physical Characteristics. Describe briefly the type of mount, cover, material from which the chart is made, etc. (see Cards 18, 19, 22, 24). When the information cannot be succinctly stated, the description of the physical characteristics should be given in a note.

The Collation statement for flannel board and magnetic board sets, which often contain a variety of parts, may include a detailed listing of the contents, if practical (see Card 22), or a notation of the number and specific designator only (see Card 23).

SERIES (Area 6)

(Series title; number within the series: Subseries title; number within the subseries)

Apply Basic Rules IX.A,B, p. 20.

NOTES (Area 7)

Apply Basic Rules X.A-I, p. 21.

For charts, a Summary which combines the supplementary information usually given in separate notes, may provide a sufficiently clear and brief description.

OTHER IDENTIFYING AND ORGANIZATIONAL DATA (Area 8)

Apply Basic Rules XI.A-E, p. 24.

D. Media Code. All charts may be coded under the general designator coding for charts, "CA", or each format may be coded separately under the coding for the specific designator.

Chart	CH
Flannel board set	CL
Flip chart	CF
Graph	CG
Magnetic board set	CM
Relief chart	CR
Wall chart	CW

```
909     An Illustrated chart showing the 5000 years of
ILL        the history of mankind.  [Chart]  Book Enter-
           prises, c1961.
           1 chart: col; 89 x 122 cm.


        CIVILIZATION, ANCIENT/ HISTORY, ANCIENT
```

CARD 16
Chart.
Title main entry.
Place omitted.

```
CA
581.3   Nystrom botany charts.  [Chart]  Developed by
NYS        Harriet B. Creighton; illus. by Natalie H.
           Davis and Martha M. Gordon.  Nystrom, [196-]
           12 charts: col; 160 x 132 cm.
           The life histories of various plants are de-
        picted in a spiral layout that emphasizes the
        cyclical nature of growth and reproduction.

        BOTANY/ GROWTH (PLANTS)/ Creighton, Harriet B./
        Davis, Natalie H./ Gordon, Martha M.
```

CARD 17
Set of charts.
Series title main entry.
General medium code in call number.
Statement of creator responsibility.

```
591.1   Jurica, Hilary S.
JUR-14     Zoology charts.  No. 14, Birds and their
        tools.  [Chart]  Developed by Dr. Hilary S.
        Jurica.  Chicago: Nystrom, [196-?]
           1 chart: col; 122 x 92 cm; folded in cover.
           Illustrates the anatomy and maturation of
        birds and how they are equipped for survival.


        BIRDS/ t: Birds and their tools./ t
```

CARD 18
One chart from a set.
Creator main entry.
Statement of creator responsibility.

```
551.6   Climagraph.  [Chart]  Hubbard, [196-]
CLI        1 graph: col; 127 x 113 cm; mounted with
        metal rods and hangers.
           With study guide.
           A chalk-markable wall chart.  Includes an
        outline world map and two graphs for plotting
        comparative monthly temperatures and precipita-
        tion throughout the world.


        CLIMATE
```

CARD 19
Graph.
Title main entry.
Place omitted.

```
CF
616.9   V.D.: then, now, and you.  [Chart]  Beverly
VEN        Hills, CA: American Educational Films, c1973.
           12 flip charts; col; 36 x 56 cm.  J-A.
           With 25 coordinated student booklets.
           Symptoms and effects of gonorrhea and syphilis
        are outlined with notation of history and current
        statistics.


        VENEREAL DISEASES
```

CARD 20
Flip charts.
Set title main entry.
Specific medium code in call number.
Educational level note.

523.3 Moon chart. [Chart] Maplewood, NJ: Hammond,
MOO [197-]
1 wall chart: col; 61 x 97 cm.
A detailed chart of the near and far sides of the moon with explanatory facts.

MOON

CA:CW

CARD 21
Wall chart.
Title main entry.
Medium code at bottom of card.

398.2 Story kits. [Chart] Springfield, MA: Milton
STO Bradley, c1967.
1 flannel board set: 8 boards, 31 x 23 cm; removable pieces, col; in cardboard box. (Flannel board teaching aids) K-P.
Guide printed on inside of cover.
A presentation of Goldilocks and the three bears, and The three little pigs. By manipulating the figures, children learn story sequence.
FOLKLORE/ t: Goldilocks and the three bears./
t: The three little pigs.

CARD 22
Flannel board set.
Title main entry.

428 Magnetic capitals assortment. [Chart] Instructo
MAG Corp., c1968.
1 magnetic board set.
Magnetized 3-dimensional capital letters and punctuation marks, 2 inches high, for use on a magnetic board. For teaching letter recognition, vocabulary, phonics, and other language arts skills.

ALPHABET/ ENGLISH LANGUAGE- STUDY AND TEACHING

CARD 23
Magnetic board set.
Title main entry.
Physical description in a note.

912 Map symbols and geographic concepts program.
GEO-1 Part A, Geographical terms model. [Chart] Nystrom, [196-?]
1 relief chart: col; 112 x 107 cm; markable vinyl surface.
With teacher's guide and 35 desk-size paper reproductions.
Shows the major landforms of the west coast of an imaginary continent, illustrating 116 geographical terms.
MAPS/ PHYSICAL GEOGRAPHY/ t: Geographical terms model.

CARD 24
Relief chart.
Series title main entry.

Medium Designator: **DIORAMA**

Specific Designator:
Diorama

Description
A *diorama* is a three-dimensional representation of a scene.

MAIN ENTRY (Area 1)

Apply Basic Rule IV.A, p. 4.

A. Title Main Entry. A diorama is entered under its title. The conditions that would warrant series title or creator main entry (see Basic Rules IV.B,C, p. 5) rarely exist for dioramas.

TITLE/MEDIUM DESIGNATOR/STATEMENT OF CREATOR RESPONSIBILITY (Area 2)

A. Title. Apply Basic Rules V.A1-10, p. 7. The title is generally taken from the box in which the diorama is stored. If the container does not provide adequate information, the title may be taken from accompanying material such as the teacher's guide, or from the producer's catalog. If variation occurs, the title on accompanying material is preferred. If no title is found, a title that is descriptive of the scene portrayed by the diorama may be supplied by the cataloger and enclosed in brackets.

B. Medium Designator. Apply Basic Rule V.B1, p. 10. The general physical form designator (medium designator) "Diorama" is given in the singular form following the Title statement and is usually enclosed in square brackets. The brackets may be omitted.

C. Statement of Creator Responsibility. The statement of creator responsibility is given only when there is no doubt as to responsibility for conception and design, and the information contributes to the identification of the diorama (see Card 25).

EDITION (Area 3)

No edition statement should be needed. Dioramas are not issued in different "editions".

IMPRINT (Area 4)*

Place: Producer, copyright/production date.

Apply Basic Rules VII.A-C, p. 15. Sponsors and distributors are seldom involved in the production and release of dioramas.

COLLATION (PHYSICAL DESCRIPTION) (Area 5)

1 diorama: number and names of parts/various pieces; color/black and white; description of container, height × width × depth of container in centimeters.

A. Number of Items and Specific Designator
1 diorama:

One diorama only is described in each entry. In simplified cataloging, the number and the specific designator, which is the same as the general designator, may be omitted (see Card 27).

B. Physical Contents. If practical, a brief listing of the number and names of the parts contained in the diorama may be recorded. When a long list or detailed description is required, the phrase "various pieces" is substituted for the enumeration in the Collation statement and the parts are described in a note.

E. Color Statement. The abbreviation "col." is used if the parts are in color, "b&w" if the parts are in black and white.

F. Size. If readily available, give the height × width × depth of the assembled diorama in centimeters, using the abbreviation "cm."

J. Other Physical Characteristics. Give a brief description and the dimensions (height × width × depth in centimeters) of the container. This information may be omitted except when the physical properties of the container are an integral part of the diorama, or they are necessary to indicate location (see Cards 26, 27).

SERIES (Area 6)

(Series title; number within the series)

Apply Basic Rule IX, p. 20. Dioramas are not usually issued in more than one series or in subseries.

*The first statement under Imprint, Collation, and Series, shows all the elements in each area as they would be recorded on the catalog card.

NOTES (Area 7)

Apply Basic Rules X.A-I, p. 21.

For dioramas, a Summary which combines the supplementary information usually given in separate notes may provide a sufficiently clear and brief description.

OTHER IDENTIFYING AND ORGANIZATIONAL DATA (Area 8)

Apply Basic Rules XI.A-E, p. 24.

D. Media Code. All dioramas may be coded under the general designator coding for dioramas, "OA", or under the specific designator coding "OD". Should new distinctive formats of dioramas be developed, additional specific designators and codings may be added.

```
OA
591     A Trip to the zoo.  [Diorama]  Created by the
TRI        fourth grade class of Washington Elementary
           School, Berkeley, CA.  Berkeley Unified School
           District, 1967.
           1 diorama: various pieces; col; in hinged
        masonite box, 30 x 25 x 13 cm.  K-P.
           Illustrations of animals and background
        scenery, with plywood stands, may be rearranged
        to create various scenes of animals at the zoo.

        ZOOLOGICAL GARDENS
```

CARD 25
Diorama.
Title main entry.
General medium code in call number.
Statement of creator responsibility.
Production date.
Educational level note.

```
OD
915.4   A Village in India.  [Diorama]  Philadelphia:
VIL        DCA Educational Products, [197-]
           1 diorama: col.  (Daily dioramas)
           Contains a small stage, 5 foreground trans-
        parencies, 2 backgrounds, 5 story sheets, and
        an easel.


        INDIA- DESCRIPTION AND TRAVEL/ ser
```

CARD 26
Diorama.
Title main entry.
Specific medium code in call number.
Physical description in a note.

```
372.6   Creating stories.  Diorama.  Instructo, [196-]
CRE        various pieces; col.  Primary.
           Contains stand-up characters, animals, and
        scenery which children can use to create and
        retell stories about fairyland, pirates, haunted
        houses, and space travel.  Designed for building
        vocabulary and story sequence skills.


        ENGLISH LANGUAGE- STUDY AND TEACHING/ STORY-
        TELLING

                                             OA:OD
```

CARD 27
Diorama.
Title main entry.
Simplified cataloging.
Medium code at bottom of card.
Medium designator.
Probable date.

Medium Designator: **FILMSTRIP**

Specific Designators:
Filmslip
Filmstrip

Description

A *filmstrip* is a roll of film, usually 35 millimeters wide, on which there is a succession of still pictures intended for projection one at a time. In a *silent filmstrip* the text may be provided by captions printed on the frames or by an accompanying script. In a *sound filmstrip* the sound track is usually recorded separately on a disc, or on a tape in cassette or reel format. Sound and frames are synchronized, with or without audible signals, for use in manual or automatic advance projectors. A *filmslip* is a short filmstrip, often in rigid format, and usually without sound accompaniment.

Specific Designators

Specific designators for formats that are experimental or require special projection equipment are not listed. Specific designators for such filmstrips may be formulated by the cataloger as needed. Caution should be exercised, however, in assigning specific designators for filmstrips in non-standard formats. As a general rule, the adoption of an additional specific designator should be delayed until the need for it is indicated by a relatively wide acceptance and distribution of a format. In many instances the format may be adequately described by using an existing specific designator and noting other physical characteristics in the Collation and/or in the Extension of physical description note.

Cartridge filmstrip
1 filmstrip: 85 fr; col; 35mm; in cartridge. (Collation)
Requires Bell &Howell cartridge load projector.
(Extension of physical description note)

Tape-cartridge filmstrip
1 filmstrip: 250 fr; col; 16mm; in cartridge with audiotape, 20 min. (Collation)
Commpak permanently synchronized film and tape cartridge.
(Extension of physical description note)

MAIN ENTRY (Area 1)

Apply Basic Rules IV.A-C, p. 4.

A. Title Main Entry. A filmstrip is generally entered under its title. If two or more filmstrips without a collective title are synchronized with sound recorded on only one disc or tape, the filmstrips are treated as a unit and are entered under the title of the first filmstrip on side one of the recording. An added entry is made for each of the titles of the other filmstrips (see Card 47).

B. Series Title Main Entry. Producers and distributors very often group filmstrips together in sets. Even though a set may not completely meet the requirements of the definition of a series, it has become common practice to use the terms *set* and *series* synonomously.

Filmstrips may be entered under the series or subseries title if easier access to the material is thus obtained. When a single filmstrip is entered under the series title, its title becomes a subtitle to the series title. An added entry is made for the title of the individual filmstrip if it is distinctive (see Cards 35, 36).

When several filmstrips are entered collectively under the series title, the titles of the individual filmstrips are given in the Contents note (see Cards 32, 32A, 33, 37, 49, 49A). Added entries are made for the titles of the individual filmstrips if they are distinctive (see Cards 33, 34).

Since producers and distributors group, package, and sell filmstrips in such a wide variety of combinations, several different conditions may determine the advisability of using series title main entry. The cataloger should consult Basic Rules IV.B1, 2, 3, p. 5, for guidance in deciding when to make main entry under series title.

C. Creator Main Entry. A filmstrip may be entered under the name of the creator if the overall responsibility for the intellectual and artistic content can be attributed to a person or corporate body, and *the name is significant in identifying the work.* An added entry is made for the title (see Cards 38, 39). When there is a shared creative responsibility by two or more persons, entry may be made under the name of the first creator listed. Added entries may be made for the other creators.

Care should be exercised in determining if authors, consultants, etc., cited either on the material itself, in the accompanying guide, or in producers' literature, are the real creators of the filmstrip. For example, the author of a study guide or of the text that appears as captions on the filmstrip frames need not be the primary creator of the work. Where there is doubt as to the creative responsibility and the identifying significance of the person or body cited, the filmstrip is entered under title (see Cards 28, 42, 47, 48). An added entry may be made for the name(s) cited (see Cards 37, 42).

A filmstrip which is an exact reproduction of a work originally produced in another medium and cataloged under the name of the creator is entered in the same manner as the original work. If the exactness of the reproduction is in doubt, and a lengthy comparison would be required for verification, the filmstrip is entered under title, and the name of the creator of the original work is given in the Statement of creator responsibility (see Card 40) or in a note. An added entry may be made for the original creator (see Card 40) or for the creator and title of the work on which the filmstrip is based. If the original work is a book or musical composition, media centers that wish to keep together all formats and interpretations of a person's work may perfer to enter the filmstrip under the name of the author or composer even though that person is not really the creator of the filmstrip (see Card 41).

TITLE/MEDIUM DESIGNATOR/STATEMENT OF CREATOR RESPONSIBILITY (Area 2)

A. Title. Apply Basic Rules V.A1-10, p. 7. The title is taken from the title frame that most closely precedes the content frames of the filmstrip. Variant titles which appear on the filmstrip, the accompanying material, or the container, and other titles under which the filmstrip may be known, may be given in a note, and added entries may be made for them. If no title is shown on the filmstrip, accompanying material, or container, the title may be taken from the producer's catalog or other reference work and the source be given in a note.

Title from producer's literature.
Title from a review.

If no title can be found, one that is indicative of the subject content of the work may be devised by the cataloger and enclosed in brackets.

When two or more filmstrips without a collective title are synchronized with sound recorded on only one disc or tape and are cataloged as a single entry, the Title statement includes the titles of all the filmstrips on the recording (see Card 47). If such a listing makes the Title statement too long, titles subsequent to the first one may be given in a note. However, if each filmstrip is cataloged separately, the titles of the other filmstrips on the audiorecording are not given in the Title statement but are indicated in a note (see Card 48).

B. Medium Designator. Apply Basic Rule V.B1, p. 10. The general physical form designator (medium designator) "Filmstrip" is given in the singular form following the Title statement and is usually enclosed in square brackets. The brackets may be omitted (see Cards 30, 44).

C. Statement of Creator Responsibility. Apply Basic Rule V.C, p. 13. The function(s) performed and the name(s) of creators such as authors, editors, consultants, collaborators, photographers, and producers, may be cited *if they are significant in identifying the work* (see Cards 28, 29, 31, 37-42, 47, 48). Added entries may be made for names cited, as considered necessary (see Cards 37, 40-42).

EDITION (Area 3)

Apply Basic Rule VI, p. 14. If a filmstrip has been revised without a change in title, the new edition is designated as it appears on the work itself, after the Medium designator/statement of creator responsibility (see Card 45). If the title has been changed in the new edition, the Edition statement is omitted. The original title and other edition information are given in a note (see Card 46).

First edition produced under the title . . .
Revised edition of the filmstrip entitled . . .
A revision of . . .

An added entry may be made for the title of the previous edition.

IMPRINT (Area 4)*

Place: Producer, copyright/production date; sponsored by Sponsor; Place: Distributed/Released by Distributor, release date.

A. Place. Apply Basic Rule VII.A, p. 15. The city of the principal offices of the producer and distributor is noted. Place is not given for a sponsor. The city and state (in the U.S.) or country (outside the U.S.) are given if there may be doubt as to the location of the city. Abbreviations of State names recommended by the U.S. Postal Service are used (see Appendix IV).†

Red Deer, Canada: Alberta Grain Growers Cooperative, c1972.

Only the name of the city is noted if it is well known.

London: Common Ground, c1969.

If the location is unknown, the probable place followed by a question mark [New York?] or the abbreviation "[s.l.]" may be noted; or place may be omitted from the Imprint statement (see Cards 30, 32, 37, 44) except where the producer or distributor is located in a country other than that of the cataloging agency.

London: Visual Publications, c1970; Distributed by
McIntyre Visual Publications, 1971.

B. Producer/Sponsor/Distributor. Apply Basic Rules VII.B1-4, p. 16. The name(s) of the producer/sponsor/distributor, as applicable, is given in the briefest form in which it can be understood and identified without ambiguity (see Cards 47-49). Phrases denoting the function of sponsor and distributor are used as explained in Basic Rules VII.B1-3 (see Card 39). The phrase "Distributed by" or "Released by" which indicates the function of the distributor may be omitted, if desired.

---

*The first statement under Imprint, Collation, and Series, shows all the elements in each area as they would be recorded on the catalog card.

†The ALA Catalog Code Revision Committee has reversed its decision to use the U.S. Postal Service State abbreviations and is now recommending that the list as given in the current *AACR* (Mass., Conn., etc.) be used in the second edition.

London: Visual Publications, c1970; New York: McIntyre Visual Publications, 1971.

The abbreviation "[s.n.]" is used if a producer, sponsor, or distributor cannot be ascertained.

C. Date. Apply Basic Rules VII.C1-4, p. 17. A date is always given, the latest copyright date taking preference over all other dates. The letter "c" preceding the date designates a copyright date. The copyright, production, and release dates after the producer and distributor, and a probable date, are recorded in accordance with Basic Rule VII.C4. The abbreviation "n.d." signifying no indication of date should not be used.

COLLATION (PHYSICAL DESCRIPTION) (Area 5)

Number of filmstrip(s)/filmslip(s): number of frames; color/black and white; 35mm & number (and) specific designator of audio accompaniment(s): physical description of accompaniment(s); other physical characteristics.

A. Number of Items and Specific Designator

1 filmstrip: 3 filmstrips: 12 filmstrips:

In simplified cataloging, if the entry describes only one filmstrip, the number and the specific designator "filmstrip" may be omitted since it is the same as the general designator. The physical description begins with the number of frames (see Cards 30, 40, 41).

C. Length. Give the number of frames using the abbreviation "fr." for single frames, "double fr." for double frames. When the horizontal axis of the picture is perpendicular to the sprocket holes the filmstrip is single-frame; when it is parallel to the sprocket holes the filmstrip is double-frame.

1. *Determination of the number of frames.* There are several methods for determining the number of frames in a filmstrip.

a) Frames numbered. If the frames are numbered, give the number that appears on the last numbered frame.

b) Frames unnumbered.

1) The number may be taken from sources other than the filmstrip itself, such as guides, producers' catalogs, reviews, and reference works.

2) The number may be determined by counting the frames. The count begins with the first content frame and ends with the last content frame. The total does not include the frames preceding or following the content frames.

3) The number may be derived by measuring from the first to the last content frame and using the formula: length (in inches) × # of frames in 12 inches ÷ 12. There are 16 frames to 12 inches of single-frame filmstrip. The resulting total is rounded off to the next larger number.

$$64 \times \frac{16}{12} = 85.33, \text{ i.e., } 86 \text{ frames}$$

Counting the number of frames in a filmstrip is time-consuming and often impractical. If length information is not considered sufficiently important to warrant expending the time to determine it, an approximate number of frames may be given followed by the abbreviation "approx.", e.g., 58 fr. approx.; or the number of frames may be omitted entirely (see Card 37).

2. *Notation of the number of frames.*

a) When the entry is for a single filmstrip give the number of frames: 35 fr. 30 double fr.

b) When the entry is for two or more filmstrips the notation may vary:

35 fr. each	Each filmstrip has the same number of frames
32, 35 fr.	Two filmstrips, each with a different number of frames
32-45 fr.	Three or more filmstrips with various numbers of frames. Give the span of the number of frames from the shortest to the longest filmstrip
178 fr.	Total the number of frames for all filmstrips in the entry

Omit the number of frames from the Collation area and record it after the title of each filmstrip in the Contents note (see Card 32).

E. Color Statement. The abbreviations "col.", "b&w", and "col. and b&w" are used to indicate that the work is in color, black and white, or a combination of color and black and white.

F. Size. Give the film width in millimeters using the abbreviation "mm". Since the majority of filmstrips are 35mm, the size may be omitted (see Cards 30, 40, 41, 44). However, if the filmstrip is other than 35mm, the size must be noted.

1 filmstrip: 180 fr; col; 16mm.

I. Accompaniments

1. *Audio accompaniment.* The sound for a filmstrip is usually provided by a separate audiorecording which is issued with the filmstrip and is considered a dependent work or integral accompaniment. The description of the audiorecording, preceded by "&", is given after the notation of size. The information includes the number of items, the specific designator, the physical description, and other pertinent identifying facts which can be stated succinctly, and is noted as prescribed in the Collation for the particular format of audiorecording (see Audiorecording, p. 39, and Cards 32-34, 38, 43, 46-48).

a) *Specific designator of audio accompaniment.* To avoid ambiguity in medium, the combining form "audio" is usually added to the specific designator.

2 filmstrips: 102 fr; col; 35mm & 2 audiodiscs:

However, the specific designator may be used without the combining form since it is generally understood that the accompaniment to a filmstrip is in the audio medium.

2 filmstrips: 102 fr; col; 35mm & 2 discs:

b) *Number of audio accompaniments.* When there is only one audiorecording the number may be omitted (see Cards 35, 36, 40, 41, 44, 45).

1 filmstrip: 58 fr; col; 35mm & audiocassette:

However, the number "1" should be noted when the audiorecording is an accompaniment to more than one filmstrip.

2 filmstrips: 45 fr. each; col; 35mm & 1 cassette:
(or 1 audiocassette)

c) *Physical description of audio accompaniment.* Time duration, if readily available, is always given. In accordance with the cataloging policy of the particular resource center, other physical description details may be completely or partially noted; or they may be omitted entirely, except when they indicate the necessity for a special kind of equipment.

8 filmstrips: col; 35mm & 8 audiocassettes: 1⅞ ips.
(Time unknown; playback speed included. See Card 32.)

5 filmstrips: 57-76 fr; col; 35mm & 5 audiodiscs, 7 in:
33.3 rpm. (Time unknown; complete physical description. See Cards 32-36.)

1 filmstrip: 32 fr; col; 35mm & cassette: 10 min.
(Time duration; other details omitted. See Cards 38, 44, 47, 48.)

1 filmstrip: 25 fr; col; 35mm & audiodisc.
(Time unknown; other details omitted. See Cards 40, 41, 45.)

2 filmstrips: 60 fr; col; 35mm & 1 audioreel, 5 in: 18 min; 3.75 ips. (Time duration; complete physical description.)

1 filmstrip: 118 fr; col; 35mm & 1 audiodisc, 12 in. (30 cm.): 12 min; 33.3 rpm. (Time duration; complete physical description with metric conversion. See Card 43.)

1) Notation of time. Time is given in minutes. Seconds are rounded off to the nearest minute; 30 seconds is counted as an extra minute. The notation pattern for time and frame length should be consistent:

When the entry is for a single filmstrip and a single recording:

35 fr. . . . 6 min.

When the entry is for two or more filmstrips and one or more recordings, the notation may vary:

35 fr. each . . . 6 min. each side. (Each filmstrip has the same number of frames and the same time duration, and each side of the recording contains the sound for a single filmstrip.)

32, 35 fr. . . . 6, 7 min. (Two filmstrips, each with a different number of frames and time duration, and each side of the recording contains the sound for a single filmstrip.)

32-45 fr. . . . 6-9 min. (Three or more filmstrips with various numbers of frames and time durations. Give the span of time from the shortest to the longest filmstrip.)

178 fr. . . . 32 min. (Total the time for all filmstrips in the entry.)

Omit the time in the Collation area and record it after the title and the number of frames of each filmstrip in the Contents note.

CONTENTS: Dante, 69 fr, 13 min.— Giotto, 86 fr, 12 min.

d) *Other physical characteristics of audio accompaniment.* If applicable, and considered important to the user, sound synchronization information may be included in the physical description of the audio accompaniment (see Cards 43, 46).

for manual or automatic projector.
1 s. for manual projector, 1 s. for automatic projector.
audible and inaudible signals.

2. *Other accompaniment.* Filmslips are often intended for individualized viewing and are designed to be used with a special hand-viewer which is issued with the filmslips. Such a device is considered an integral accompaniment and its description, preceded by "&", is given following the width of the film (see Card 49).

J. Other Physical Characteristics. Give a brief description of other physical characteristics that may be pertinent to the utilization or storage of the filmstrip(s), such as special format, shelving or shipping container, etc.

in cartridge
in plastic container, 30 × 25 × 5 cm.

When the information cannot be succinctly stated, the description of these physical properties should be given in a note instead of in the Collation (see Extension of Physical Description).

SERIES (Area 6)

(Series title; number within the series: Subseries title; number within the subseries)

Apply Basic Rules IX.A,B, p. 20. Give the series title in parentheses following the Collation *in the form in which it appears on the work itself* (see Cards 28-31, 33-36, 38, 43, 44, 47, 48). The series title may appear on the individual title frame, on a frame that precedes the individual title frame, or at the end of the filmstrip. The series title should not be taken from the filmstrip container or the container in which the several filmstrips in a set or series are packaged, or from vendors' and producers' catalogs. For promotional purposes, filmstrips may often be presented under new series titles or be regrouped into several different sets, and vendors' series titles may differ from those of the producer. A series title which is not shown on the filmstrip itself but appears prominently on its container may be given in a note if the work may be known or requested under that series title. An added entry may be made for it, if desired.

Series title on container: Vertebrates and invertebrates.

If a series title is taken from a source other than the filmstrip itself and is recorded in the Series area, the source is given in a note.

Series title from container.
Series title from shipping container.

When main entry is under series title, the Series statement is omitted unless the filmstrip(s) is part of another series, or is a subseries (see Cards 33-36).

NOTES (Area 7)

Apply Basic Rules X.A-I, p. 21. Notes are designed to provide supplementary information about the filmstrip not brought out in the formal description. They should be as brief as clarity and good grammar permit, and may be combined or grouped together to create a clear informational and descriptive statement. The choice of notes and the fullness of detail will vary according to the needs of the particular clientele.

A. Educational Level. If desired, the educational level for which the filmstrip is intended may be noted following the Series statement. The terms or abbreviations given in Basic Rule X.A are used (see Cards 28, 29, 31, 33-37, 40, 41, 45, 49). Or, the educational level, audience suitability and/or restrictions may be described in the Summary (see Card 46).

B. Extension of Physical Description. Give any additional information required for a more complete description of the physical properties of the filmstrip.

3 of the 6 filmstrips are synchronized with audiocassette.

Synchronized film and audiotape permanently enclosed in cartridge.

If the filmstrip cannot be projected by a standard projector, give sufficient information to identify the equipment required.

For use with Bell & Howell cartridge projector.

Swivelling projector required for images placed in frames horizontally and vertically.

C. Accompanying and/or Descriptive Material. Describe material designed to assist in the understanding of the filmstrip(s) in brief and specific terms. The descriptor may be a commonly used term or phrase such as teacher's guide, manual, etc., or it may be transcribed from the material itself. Additional bibliographic information such as title, author, and pagination of accompanying material, if readily available, may also be given. Such information, and the beginning preposition "With" may be omitted in simplified cataloging.

With teacher's guide/ instructor's guide/ discussion guide/ series guide/ etc.

With teacher's guide and description of frames.

Teacher's guide and script.

With picture-cued text.

Text booklet.
Study guide by Eugene H. White.
With manual. 10 p.
With paperback book entitled A field guide to western birds, by Roger T. Peterson. 97 p.

Captions. This information may be given in the Summary as an introductory phrase or a concluding statement.

Captioned drawings portray the daily activities of young children in kindergarten.
Presents scenes from the daily lives of children in Peru. Captions.

D. Other Versions. Each version of a filmstrip in the collection is cataloged separately. To minimize repetitive cataloging, the various versions in the collection may be listed on one card. Give sufficient information to identify differences in physical characteristics and location.

Other versions in the same or a different medium that are not in the collection and are known to exist may be noted (see Cards 38, 46-48).

Also issued as a 16mm motion picture.
Also issued as a slide set with audiocassette.

F. Related Works. Cite works upon which the filmstrip depends for its intellectual and/or artistic content (see Cards 32, 43) or with which it is correlated, and make appropriate added entries.

Each filmstrip is correlated with a reader in the textbook series Reading for fun.
Correlated with the textbook of the same title.

G. Credits. Give the names of individuals and organizations whose contributions in creating the filmstrip are considered significant and who have not been noted in the Statement of creator responsibility. Authors of captions, scripts, or guides, educational consultants, collaborators, demonstrators, photographers, narrators, and producers may be cited. Note the function or contribution, followed by the name, and make added entries as considered necessary (see Cards 32, 43, 49). The caption "CREDITS" may be omitted.

H. Summary. Provide a brief statement of the subject content of the filmstrip if it is not evident from the title. Supplementary information discussed under other notes may often be combined in the Summary statement. The caption "SUMMARY" may be omitted.

I. Contents. When a work consists of a number of parts, or an entry includes several filmstrips, each of which has a distinctive title, record these titles in the Contents note. If the titles are so numerous that a complete listing is impractical, a partial listing may suffice, or the Contents note may be omitted in favor of an informal listing included in the Summary statement. The number of frames and the time duration of each filmstrip may be noted after its title (see Notation of the Number of Frames, Notation of Time, and Card 32). The caption "CONTENTS" or "PARTIAL CONTENTS" may be omitted.

When two or more filmstrips without a collective title are synchronized with sound recorded on only one disc or tape and each filmstrip is cataloged as a separate entry, note the title(s) of the other filmstrip(s) for which the audiorecording is an accompaniment (see Card 48).

OTHER IDENTIFYING AND ORGANIZATIONAL DATA (Area 8)

Apply Basic Rules XI.A-E, p. 24.

C. Classification Number. Filmstrips may be organized by subject content and classified by the Library of Congress or Dewey Decimal systems to achieve subject integration with books and other audiovisual materials. The shape and size of filmstrips and their audio accompaniments, the provision of only one guide for several filmstrips, and the lack of uniformity in packaging make the integrated shelving of filmstrips difficult. Consequently, they are often kept together in a separate area in cabinets or on shelves designed specifically for filmstrip storage. Subject classification permits an orderly arrangement in such collections. However, if classification is intended only as a locator, a simple sequential accession numbering system may be preferred (see Cards 43, 44).

D. Media Code. Automated procedures generally require that medium designators be coded. The same code should be used in manual systems if codification is desired. For informational purposes, the coding for the general and specific designators may be shown at the bottom of the shelf list and/or catalog card (see Card 39).

1. *General and specific designator code.* All filmstrips may be coded under the general designator coding for filmstrips "FA", or each format may be coded separately under the coding for its specific designator.

Filmstrip	FS
Filmslip	FL

2. *Media code and designators in the call number.* When filmstrips are stored in a separate area, the medium coding or designator may be placed above the classification number to serve as a location device. The decision to use the general or specific designator spelled out in full or the medium coding will depend upon the requirements of the patrons served and of the particular automated or manual system, the size of the collection, and the storage facilities.

3. *Color code.* The color coding of catalog cards to indicate that the work is a filmstrip or is in a nonbook format is _not_ recommended.

```
FS
973.1   Discoverers of the Great Lakes: Frenchmen in
DIS        America.  [Filmstrip]  Author, J.W. Todd.
           Mahwah, NJ: Troll Associates, c1968.
           1 filmstrip: 45 fr.; col.; 35mm.  (Great
        explorers)  I-J.
           SUMMARY: Discusses the explorations of Cartier,
        Champlain, Marquette, and LaSalle.  With cap-
        tions.

        EXPLORERS, FRENCH/ GREAT LAKES- DISCOVERY AND
        EXPLORATION/ ser
```

CARD 28
Filmstrip.
Title main entry.
Fully detailed cataloging.
Specific medium code in call number.

```
FA
973.1   Discoverers of the Great Lakes: Frenchmen in
DIS        America.  [Filmstrip]  Author, J.W. Todd.
           Troll Associates, c1968.
           filmstrip: 45 fr; col; 35mm.  (Great ex-
        plorers)  I-J.
           Discusses the explorations of Cartier,
        Champlain, Marquette, and LaSalle.  Captions.


        EXPLORERS, FRENCH/ GREAT LAKES- DISCOVERY AND
        EXPLORATION/ ser
```

CARD 29
Filmstrip.
Title main entry.
Moderately detailed cataloging.
General medium code in call number.
Place, number of items (1) omitted.

```
Filmstrip

973.1   Discoverers of the Great Lakes: Frenchmen in
DIS        America.  Filmstrip.  Troll Associates,
           c1968.
           45 fr; col.  (Great explorers)
           Captions.


        EXPLORERS, FRENCH/ GREAT LAKES- DISCOVERY AND
        EXPLORATION/ ser
```

CARD 30
Filmstrip.
Title main entry.
Simplified cataloging.
Specific designator in call number.
Medium designator without brackets.

973.1 DIS

Discoverers of the Great Lakes : Frenchmen in America / [Filmstrip] / Author, J.W. Todd. Mahwah, NJ: Troll Associates, c1968.

1 filmstrip : 45 fr. ; col. ; 35mm. - (Great explorers) - I-J.

SUMMARY: Discusses the explorations of Cartier, Champlain, Marquette, and LaSalle. With captions.

1. Explorers, French. 2. Great Lakes - Discovery and exploration. I. Series.

CARD 31
Filmstrip.
Title main entry.
ISBD punctuation.

901.9 CIV v.1

Civilisation. Vol. 1. [Filmstrip] Time-Life Films, c1971.

8 filmstrips: col; 35mm & 8 audiocassettes: 1 7/8 ips.

With teacher's guide including script.

Based on the BBC film series Civilisation.

Narrator, Kenneth Clark.

The frozen world, 75 fr.- The great thaw, 75 fr.- Romance and reality, 75 fr.- Man--the measure of all things, 76 fr.- The hero as artist, 103 fr.- Protest and communication, 89 fr.-

(See next card)

CARD 32
Filmstrip series with audio accompaniment.
Series title main entry.
Place omitted.
Time duration unknown.
Notes (captions omitted):
- **Related works.**
- **Credits.**
- **Contents, with length of each title.**

(Card 2)

901.9 Civilisation. Vol. 1. [Filmstrip]
CIV
v.1 Grandeur and obedience, 94 fr.- The pursuit of happiness, 89 fr.

CIVILIZATION/ British Broadcasting Corporation/ Clark, Kenneth.

CARD 32A
Continuation card.

155.4 Who am I? (Concept of self) [Filmstrip] Engle-
WHO wood Cliffs, NJ: Inside Out Productions, c1970.

5 filmstrips: 57-76 fr; col; 35mm & 5 audiodiscs, 7 in: 33.3 rpm. (Kindle sound-filmstrip series. Unit 1) Primary.

Designed to help the young child understand himself.

Nothing is something to do.- The joy of being you.- People packages.- All kinds of feelings.- Do you believe in wishes?

CHILD STUDY/ SELF-REALIZATION/
t: contents/ ser

CARD 33
Filmstrip set with audio accompaniment.
Subseries title main entry.
Length: Span of frames; time unknown.
Educational level note.

All kinds of feelings.

155.4 WHO

Who am I? (Concept of self) [Filmstrip] Englewood Cliffs, NJ: Inside Out Productions, c1970.

5 filmstrips: 57-76 fr; col; 35mm & 5 audiodiscs, 7 in: 33.3 rpm. (Kindle sound-filmstrip series. Unit 1) Primary.

Designed to help the young child understand himself.

Nothing is something to do.- The joy of being you.- People packages.- All kinds of feelings.- Do you believe in wishes?

CHILD STUDY/ SELF-REALIZATION/
t: contents/ ser

CARD 34
Title added entry for 1 filmstrip cataloged as part of a set.

155.4 WHO-4

Who am I? (Concept of self) No. 4, All kinds of feelings. [Filmstrip] Englewood Cliffs, NJ: Inside Out Productions, c1970.

1 filmstrip: 58 fr; col; 35mm & audiodisc, 7 in: 33.3 rpm. (Kindle sound-filmstrip series. Unit 1) Primary.

A story designed to help the young child understand different kinds of emotions.

EMOTIONS/ SELF-REALIZATION/ t: All kinds of feelings/ ser

CARD 35
One filmstrip from a set, cataloged individually.
Subseries title main entry.
Individual filmstrip title is a subtitle to main entry title.

All kinds of feelings.

155.4 Who am I? (Concept of self) No. 4, All kinds of
WHO-4 feelings. [Filmstrip] Englewood Cliffs, NJ:
Inside Out Productions, c1970.
1 filmstrip: 58 fr; col; 35mm & audiodisc,
7 in: 33.3 rpm. (Kindle sound-filmstrip series.
Unit 1) Primary.
A story designed to help the young child
understand different kinds of emotions.

EMOTIONS/ SELF-REALIZATION/ t: All kinds of
feelings/ ser

CARD 36
Title added entry for 1 filmstrip from a set, cataloged individually.

599 Animals. [Filmstrip] Captioned for the use of
ANI the deaf by Media Services and Captioned
Films Branch, U.S. Bureau of Education for
the Handicapped. Jack Lieb Productions, c1970.
10 filmstrips: col; 35mm. Primary.
CONTENTS: Animals.- The gorilla.- The lion.-
The giraffe.- The polar bear.- The elephant.-
What is it? (test strip).- The brown bat.- The
elephant seal.- The platypus.
ANIMALS/ MAMMALS/ U.S. Bureau of Education for
the Handicapped. Media Services and Captioned
Films Branch.

CARD 37
Filmstrip set.
Set title main entry.
Added entry for organization cited in Statement of creator responsibility.
Number of frames omitted.

629.2 Radlauer, Edward
RAD Custom cars. [Filmstrip] Written and photographed by Ed Radlauer. Glendale, CA: Bowmar, c1968.
1 filmstrip: 32 fr; col; 35mm & 1 audiocassette: 10 min. (Reading incentive program)
With teacher's guide and 10 student booklets.
Also issued with audiodisc.
Custom cars are presented as a hobby. Designed to stimulate interest in reading.
AUTOMOBILES/ READING/ t/ ser

CARD 38
Filmstrip with audio accompaniment.
Creator main entry.
Other versions note.

701 Beswick, John S.
BES The language of color. [Filmstrip] Compiled, photographed, and annotated by John S. Beswick. London: Visual Publications, c1970; Champlain, NY: Distributed by McIntyre Visual Publications, 1971.
6 filmstrips: 31-51 fr; col; 35mm.
With teacher's guide for each filmstrip.
Colour is light.- The changing world around us.- Light, form, and colour.- Some characteristics of colour. Colour illusion and abstraction.- Optical colour mixing.
COLOR/ t
FA:FS

CARD 39
Filmstrip set.
Creator main entry.
Producer & distributor.
Copyright & release dates.
Medium code at bottom of card.

KIS A Kiss for Little Bear. [Filmstrip] By Else Holmelund Minarik, with pictures by Maurice Sendak. Weston, CT: Weston Woods Studios, c1972.
34 fr; col. & audiocassette. Primary.
With picture-cued text.
Uses the text and pictures of the book to tell how Little Bear received a kiss from his grandmother.

ANIMALS- STORIES/ Minarik, Else Holmelund/ Sendak, Maurice

CARD 40
Filmstrip with audio accompaniment.
Modified reproduction of a book.
Title main entry.
Physical description of audio accompaniment omitted.

MIN Minarik, Else Holmelund
A kiss for Little Bear. [Filmstrip] Pictures by Maurice Sendak. Weston, CT: Weston Woods Studios, c1972.
34 fr; col. & audiocassette. Primary.
With picture-cued text.
Uses the text and pictures of the book to tell how Little Bear received a kiss from his grandmother.

ANIMALS- STORIES/ Sendak, Maurice/ t

CARD 41
Filmstrip with audio accompaniment.
Modified reproduction of a book.
Author main entry.

371.3 A Unit method of teaching. [Filmstrip] Prepared
UNI by Robert E. Brownlee, and others. El Cerrito,
CA: Long Filmslide Service, c1955.
2 filmstrips: 107 fr; b&w; 35mm.
SUMMARY: Captioned photographs demonstrate an approach to teaching language arts to attain skills in thinking, reading, writing, speaking, and listening.
CONTENTS: 1. Development of theme ideas.- 2. Provision for effective learning. Grouping students for effective learning.
EDUCATION- EXPERIMENTAL METHODS/ ENGLISH LANGUAGE- STUDY AND TEACHING (SECONDARY)/ Brownlee, Robert E.

CARD 42
Two filmstrips containing 3 parts.
Title main entry.
Length: total of frames in 2 filmstrips.

1050 Tradition. [Filmstrip] Chicago: Field Educational Publications, c1972.
1 filmstrip: 118 fr; col; 35mm & 1 audiodisc, 12 in.(30 cm.): 12 min; 33.3 rpm; for manual or automatic projector. (Story of Latin America)
Based on the book by Greco and Bacon.
Producers, Al Vedro, Douglas Cox; narrator, Roberto Tafur; music, Ed Wetland; photographer, Richard Crone.
Presents the Indians of the Andes as an example of the varied peoples in Latin America.
INDIANS OF SOUTH AMERICA- ANDES/ ser

CARD 43
Filmstrip with audio accompaniment.
Title main entry.
Accession number classification.
Physical description of audio accompaniment, with metric conversion.
Notes (captions omitted):
- **Related works.**
- **Credits.**
- **Summary.**

1050 Tradition. Filmstrip. Field, c1972.
118 fr; col. & audiodisc: 12 min. (Story of Latin America)
Presents the Indians of the Andes as an example of the varied peoples in Latin America.

INDIANS OF SOUTH AMERICA/ ser

CARD 44
Filmstrip with audio accompaniment.
Title main entry.
Simplified cataloging.

980 The Historic background [of South America]
HIS [Filmstrip] Rev. ed. Jamaica, NY: Eye Gate House, c1965.
1 filmstrip: 25 fr; col; 35mm & audiodisc. (South America: a regional study; no. 1) I-J.
With series guide.

SOUTH AMERICA- HISTORY/ ser

CARD 45
Filmstrip with audio accompaniment.
Title main entry.
Phrase supplied for meaningless title.
Edition statement.
Series sequence number.

612.6 Sex education in America. Part 1, 2, 3. [Film-
SEX strip] Pleasantville, NY: Guidance Associates,
c1971.
3 filmstrips: 215 fr; col; 35mm & 3 audiodiscs:
41 min; for manual or automatic projector.
With discussion guide.
Also issued with audiocassettes.
A revision of the 1968 filmstrip entitled
Sex education U.S.A.
Discusses the need for sex education, current
information, and successful curricula. For par-
ents, teachers, administrators and guid-
ance groups.
SEX INSTRUCTION- U.S./ t: Sex education U.S.A.

CARD 46
Filmstrips containing 3 parts, with audio accompaniment.
Title main entry.
Parts designated in title.
Edition note: Rev. ed. with title change.
Audience suitability.

915.2 Japan: Hiroshima and Osaka. Germany: the middle
JAP Rhine region. [Filmstrip] Developed by
Richard Flynn. Chicago: SVE, c1968.
2 filmstrips: 51, 55 fr; col; 35mm & 1 audio-
cassette: 10, 12 min. (Communities around the
world. Group 2)
With teacher's guide for each filmstrip.
Also issued with audiodisc.

GERMANY- SOCIAL LIFE AND CUSTOMS/ JAPAN- SOCIAL
LIFE AND CUSTOMS/ t: Germany ... region./ ser

CARD 47
Two filmstrips with 1 audiorecording.
Main entry under title on side 1 of recording.
Added entry for title on side 2 of recording.

915.2 Germany: the middle Rhine region. [Filmstrip]
JAP Developed by Richard Flynn. Chicago: SVE, c1968.
1 filmstrip: 55 fr; col; 35mm & 1 audiocassette: 12 min. (Communities around the world. Group 2)
With teacher's guide.
Also issued with audiodisc.
Side 1 of recording: Japan: Hiroshima and Osaka.
GERMANY- SOCIAL LIFE AND CUSTOMS/ ser

CARD 48
Two filmstrips with 1 audiorecording: filmstrip on side 2 of recording cataloged individually.
Title main entry.

FL
338.1 Food. [Filmstrip] Chicago: EBEC, c1973.
FOO 12 filmslips: 14 fr. each; col; 35mm & plastic hand-viewer. Primary.
May also be viewed with projector.
Collaborator, P. Craig Smith.
Captioned pictures trace man's efforts to provide himself with food. Includes review questions and activities.
Man needs food.- Early man's food.- The food supply grows.- Food for good health.- The grain foods.- The milk foods.- Meat and other protein

(See next card)

CARD 49
Filmslip set.
Title main entry.
Specific medium code in call number.
Accompaniment.
Extension of physical description note.

(Card 2)

FL
338.1 Food. [Filmstrip]
FOO

foods.- The fruits and vegetables.- Raising food today.- The food industry today.- Food problems today.- Solving food problems.

FOOD SUPPLY/ NUTRITION

CARD 49A
Filmslip set.
Continuation card.

Medium Designator: **FLASH CARD**

Specific Designator:
Card

Description

A *flash card* is a card or other opaque material with words, numerals or pictures designed to be displayed briefly by hand or by mechanical device for the purpose of drill or recognition training. A flash card with sound, often called an audiocard, has along its bottom edge a strip of audiotape containing up to 15 seconds of recorded sound. When inserted in an audiocard player, pictures and words are presented simultaneously. Flash cards are always issued in sets.

MAIN ENTRY (Area 1)

Apply Basic Rules IV.A-C, p. 4.

A. Title Main Entry. Entry under the title of the set is preferred for flash cards since they are usually identified by set title.

B. Series Title Main Entry. When flash card sets are issued in a series, each set is generally cataloged under its own title. The series title may be used for the main entry when the title of the individual set is dependent upon the series title for meaning, or when the various sets are not sold individually.

C. Creator Main Entry. A flash card set may be entered under the name of the creator if the overall responsibility for the conception and design can be attributed to one person or corporate body; if the name appears on the cards, the guide, or the container; and *if the name is significant in identifying the work.* An added entry is made for the title.

TITLE/MEDIUM DESIGNATOR/STATEMENT OF CREATOR RESPONSIBILITY (Area 2)

A. Title. Apply Basic Rules V.A1-10, p. 7. The title of a flash card set is taken from the cards, accompanying guides, the container, or the producer's catalog. Preference is given the title on the cards if a variation occurs. If no title is found, one may be supplied by the cataloger and shown in brackets.

B. Medium Designator. Apply Basic Rule V.B1, p. 10. The general physical form designator (medium designator) "Flash card" is given in the singular form following the Title statement and is usually enclosed in square brackets. The brackets may be omitted.

C. Statement of Creator Responsibility. Apply Basic Rule V.C, p. 13.

EDITION (Area 3)

Apply Basic Rule VI, p. 14.

IMPRINT (Area 4)*

Place: Producer, copyright/production date; sponsored by Sponsor; Place: Distributed/Released by Distributor, release date.

Apply Basic Rules VII.A-C, p. 15.

COLLATION (PHYSICAL DESCRIPTION) (Area 5)

Number of cards: color/black and white; height × width in centimeters & integral accompaniment(s); other physical characteristics.

A. Number of Items and Specific Designator

12 cards:	3 sets of cards: 12 cards each;
	3 sets of cards: 36 cards;

When the entry is for a multi-set, the number of sets is given, followed by the number of cards in each set or the total of the cards in the sets. The number of cards in the sets may be omitted from the Collation statement and recorded after the titles of the sets if they are listed in the Contents note.

E. Color Statement. The abbreviation "col." is used if the lettering and/or illustrations are printed in colored ink, "b&w" if they are printed in black ink.

F. Size. Give the height times the width of the cards in centimeters, using the abbreviation "cm."

I. Accompaniments. In some instances, flash cards are designed to be used with an accompaniment, such as a manipulative device or an audiorecording. This accompaniment is considered an integral part of the flash card set and its description, preceded by "&", is given after the dimensions (see Card 51).

---

*The first statement under Imprint, Collation, and Series, shows all the elements in each area as they would be recorded on the catalog card.

J. Other Physical Characteristics. Give a brief description of other physical characteristics that may be pertinent to the utilization or storage of the flash card set, such as the type and dimensions of the container in centimeters, peculiarities of mounting, binding, or shape (see Cards 50, 52). When the information cannot be succinctly stated, the description of these physical properties should be given in a note instead of in the Collation.

SERIES (Area 6)

(Series title; number of the set within the series: Subseries title; number of the set within the subseries)

Apply Basic Rules IX.A,B, p. 20.

NOTES (Area 7)

Apply Basic Rules X.A-I, p. 21.

B. Extension of Physical Description. Give any additional information required to convey a more complete picture of the size and physical properties of the work, or of special equipment needed to manipulate the cards.

Answers on verso of cards.
Cards printed on both sides.

For flash cards, a summary which combines the supplementary information often given in several separate notes, may provide a sufficiently clear and brief description.

OTHER IDENTIFYING AND ORGANIZATIONAL DATA (Area 8)

Apply Basic Rules XI.A-E, p. 24.

D. Media Code. All flash card sets may be coded under the general designator coding for flash cards, "HA", or under the specific designator coding "HC". Should new distinctive formats of flash cards be developed, additional specific designators and codings may be added.

```
HA
421     A Basal set of phonetic word drill cards for use
BAS-1      with any system of reading.  Set A.  [Flash
           card]  Buffalo, NY: Kenworthy Educational
           Service, c1965.
           10 cards: col; 10 x 20 cm; each hinged with
        10 x 10 cm. cards.  Primary.
           Cards printed on both sides.
           Instructions for use on container.
           The word endings on the basic cards combine
        with the initial sounds on the flip cards to
        form 272 different words.
        PHONETICS/ VOCABULARY/ t: Phonetic word
        drill cards.
```

CARD 50
Flash card set.
Title main entry.
General medium code in call number.

```
HC
513     Addition.  [Flash card]  Dallas, TX: World Re-
ADD        search Co., [197-]
           18 cards: col; 20 x 5 cm. & plastic card
        holder.  (Elementary mathematics)  P-I.
           Cards printed on both sides.
           With guide, blank cards, test and score sheets.
           Designed for individualized learning, the
        student advances the card through the holder as
        he progresses through the ten problems that are
        presented on each card.
        ADDITION/ ser
```

CARD 51
Flash card set.
Title main entry.
Specific medium code in call number.

```
421     Learn the alphabet.  [Flash card]  Springfield,
LEA        MA: Milton Bradley, c1963.
           56 cards: col. and b&w; 20 x 12 cm; in card-
        board box.  Primary.
           With guide and game instructions.
           Letter and picture cards, printed on both
        sides, may also be used for games.


        ALPHABET/ GAMES

                                                HA:HC
```

CARD 52
Flash card set.
Title main entry.
Medium code at bottom of card.

```
597     Fishes.  Flash card.  Gelleswidmer, c1962.
FIS        48 cards: col.
           Guide.


        FISHES
```

CARD 53
Flash card set.
Title main entry.
Simplified cataloging.

Medium Designator: **GAME**

Specific Designators:
Game
Puzzle
Simulation

Description

A *game* consists of a set of materials designed for competitive play according to prescribed rules and intended for recreation or instruction. A *puzzle* presents a problem that requires solution and tests problem-solving skills. A *simulation* presents a model of a real situation that requires role-playing and interaction from the players.

MAIN ENTRY (Area 1)

Apply Basic Rules IV.A-C, p. 4.

A. Title Main Entry. Title main entry is preferred since games are usually identified by title by the producer and the user.

B. Series Title Main Entry. When games are issued in a series, main entry under series title may be made in accordance with Basic Rules IV.B1-3 (see Card 55).

C. Creator Main Entry. A game may be entered under the name of the creator if the overall responsibility for the intellectual content and design can be attributed to one person or corporate body; if the name appears on the container, instructions, or guide; and *if the name is significant in identifying the work.* An added entry is made for the title.

Creator main entry may occur more frequently for simulations (see Card 57) which often consist only of teacher and student guides and whose authorship is clearly indicated.

TITLE/MEDIUM DESIGNATOR/STATEMENT OF CREATOR RESPONSIBILITY (Area 2)

A. Title. Apply Basic Rules V.A1-10, p. 7. The title is taken from the container in which the game is packaged, from instructions or other materials in the container, from accompanying guides, or from the producer's catalog. If no title is found, one may be supplied by the cataloger and shown in brackets.

B. Medium Designator. Apply Basic Rule V.B1, p. 10. The general physical form designator (medium designator) "Game" is given in the singular form following the Title statement and is usually enclosed in square brackets. The brackets may be omitted.

C. Statement of Creator Responsibility. Apply Basic Rule V.C, p. 13. (see Cards 54, 55).

EDITION (Area 3)

Apply Basic Rule VI, p. 14.

IMPRINT (Area 4)*

Place: Producer, copyright/production date; sponsored by Sponsor: Place: Distributed/Released by Distributor, release date.

Apply Basic Rules VII.A-C, p. 15.

COLLATION (PHYSICAL DESCRIPTION) (Area 5)

Number of game(s)/puzzle(s)/simulation(s): description of parts/ various pieces.

A. Number of Items and Specific Designator

1 game: 2 puzzles: 4 simulations:

In simplified cataloging, when the entry is for one game, the number and the specific designator, which is the same as the general designator, may be omitted.

B. Physical Contents. If practical, give the number, kind, and description of the parts. The description may include any of the following information that is considered pertinent to the utilization and/or storage of the game: color, sizes of pieces, playing board, container, items not included in the container, etc. No order of listing can be prescribed because of the wide variety in game components. If the game includes an inventory, the cataloger may record the items as given, or group them together in a logical or alphabetical sequence. Teacher's guides, student manuals, and instruction booklets are usually noted in the Collation statement rather than in an accompanying materials note (see Accompanying and/or Descriptive Materials). When a long list or detailed description is required, the phrase "various pieces" may be substituted for the enumeration of all or some of the items. Further description, if considered necessary, may be given in a note.

---

*The first statement under Imprint, Collation, and Series, shows all the elements in each area as they would be recorded on the catalog card.

1 game: instruction manual; playing board, b&w, 16 × 10 cm; various pieces in box, 15 × 8 cm.
4 simulations: teacher's guide; 35 student manuals.
1 game: slotted board; number wheel; cards; dice; scoring counters.
1 puzzle: various pieces.

SERIES (Area 6)

(Series title: number within the series: Subseries title: number within the subseries)

Apply Basic Rules IX.A,B, p. 20.

NOTES (Area 7)

Apply Basic Rules X.A-I, p. 21. Notes are designed to provide supplementary information about the game not brought out in the formal description. They should be as brief as clarity and good grammar permit, and may be combined and grouped together to create a logical entry. The fullness of detail will vary according to the needs of the particular clientele.

A. Educational Level. The educational level, if desired, may be indicated following the Series statement, using the designations or abbreviations recommended in Basic Rule X.A (see Card 58) or it may be included in the information given in the Summary (see Card 54).

B. Extension of Physical Description. Give any additional information required to convey a more complete picture of the physical properties of the game, or of equipment or materials needed to fully utilize the work.

Instructions on inside of container lid.
Game board printed on container.
Requires duplication of scoring sheets.
Use with a map of the United States.

C. Accompanying and/or Descriptive Material. Materials accompanying the game which are designed to assist in its presentation or understanding, such as teacher's guides, student manuals, and instruction booklets, are usually recorded in the physical description (see Collation). However, when the description of the material includes bibliographic information, it is given in a note instead of in the Collation statement.

With player's manual. 16 p.
Teacher's guide by Robert Garry Shirts. 24 p.

H. Summary. The intent of the game should be stated, and the number of players indicated. If known, the time required to play the game is also noted. The grade level may be included in the Summary if it has not been given in the Educational level note (see Card 54). The caption "SUMMARY" may be omitted.

I. Contents. If a work consists of a number of parts, or an entry includes several games, their titles are given in a Contents note (see Card 55). The caption "CONTENTS" may be omitted.

OTHER IDENTIFYING AND ORGANIZATIONAL DATA (Area 8)

Apply Basic Rules XI.A-E, p. 24.

D. Media Code. The several formats of games may be coded together under the general designator coding for games "GA", or each format may be coded separately under the coding for its specific designator.

Game	GM
Puzzle	GP
Simulation	GS

```
GA
152.4   Hang-up.  [Game]  Developed by W.J. Gordon and
HAN        T. Poze.  Cambridge, MA: Synectics Education
           Systems, c1969.
           1 game: players' manuals; playing board;
        cards; role cards; dice.
           SUMMARY: An interactive game designed to
        assist individuals to recognize their prejudices.
        3-6 players; 1 hour minimum; junior high and up.

        PREJUDICES AND ANTIPATHIES
```

CARD 54
Game.
Title main entry.
General medium code in call number.
Statement of creator responsibility.

GM
973 American history games. [Game] Developed by
AME Abt Associates, Alice K. Gordon, and others.
Chicago: Science Research Associates, c1970.
6 games: teacher's guide; spirit master book;
35 game books; playing boards; tokens; cards. J-H.
SUMMARY: Each game deals with major issues in
America's past.
CONTENTS: Colony.- Frontier.- Reconstruction.-
Promotion.- Intervention.- Development.

U.S.- HISTORY/ Abt Associates

CARD 55
Game set.
Series title main entry.
Specific medium code in call number.
Contents note.
Educational level note.

428 Interaction: Games, level 2: Silly syntax set.
INT [Game] Houghton Mifflin, c1973.
1 game: 3 decks of playing cards; charts;
activity cards.
A component in a student-centered language
arts and reading program by James Moffett.
Designed to help students develop an understanding of sentence construction and the parts
of speech.
ENGLISH LANGUAGE- GRAMMAR/ Moffet, James/
t: Silly syntax set.

CARD 56
Game: part of a kit.
Kit title main entry.
Related works note.
Place omitted.

342.73 Rothschild, Eric
ROT 1787. [Game] Hartsdale, NY: Olcott Forward, c1970.
1 simulation: administrator's manual; 1 disc, 12 in, 33.3 rpm; 4 duplicating masters; delegate handbooks and profile cards; wall chart. J-H.
A simulation of the Constitutional Convention in which players act out the roles of real people. Designed to familiarize students with how delegates draft, adopt, and support a constitution.
U.S.- CONSTITUTIONAL HISTORY/ t

CARD 57
Simulation.
Creator main entry.

917.3 United States map puzzle. [Game] Springfield,
UNI MA: Playskool/Milton Bradley, c1971.
1 puzzle: 49 pieces, col; wood tray, 31 x 51 cm. Primary.
Scale 160 miles:1 in.
Informational notes about each State printed on verso of pieces.

U.S.- MAPS

GA:GP

CARD 58
Puzzle.
Title main entry.
Medium code at bottom of card.

Medium Designator: **GLOBE**

Specific Designators:
Globe
Relief globe

Description

A *globe* is a sphere upon which is depicted a map of the earth (terrestrial globe) or of the heavens (celestial globe), showing the elements in their relative size and/or proper relationships. A *relief globe* shows the earth's contours in raised surfaces.

MAIN ENTRY (Area 1)

Apply Basic Rules IV.A-C, p. 4.

A. Title Main Entry. Title entry is usually preferred for globes. The name of the producer may often occur as the initial word in the title (see Card 60).

B. Series Main Entry. When globes are issued in a series, each globe is generally cataloged under its own title.

C. Creator Main Entry. Main entry may be made under the cartographer's name *if it is significant in identifying the globe.* Commercial firms that produce globes are not considered for main entry. The producer's name may, however, appear as the initial word in a title main entry (see Card 60).

TITLE/MEDIUM DESIGNATOR/STATEMENT OF CREATOR RESPONSIBILITY (Area 2)

A. Title. Apply Basic Rules V.A1-10, p. 7. The title is taken from the globe itself. It may appear anywhere on the surface of the globe, either scattered or in an insert. In some cases the only title will be on a tag attached by the manufacturer. If no suitable title is found, one may be supplied by the cataloger and shown in brackets.

B. Medium Designator. Apply Basic Rule V.B1, p. 10. The general physical form designator (medium designator) "Globe" is given in the singular form following the Title statement and is usually enclosed in square brackets. The brackets may be omitted.

C. Statement of Creator Responsibility. Apply Basic Rule V.C, p. 13. The name(s) of the cartographer(s) and/or other person(s) responsible for researching the data needed to create the globe may be stated after the medium designator *if they are significant in identifying the work,* and added entries may be made, as needed (see Card 62).

EDITION (Area 3)

Apply Basic Rule VI, p. 14.

IMPRINT (Area 4)*

Place: Producer, copyright/production date; sponsored by Sponsor; Place: Distributed/Released by Distributor, release date.

Apply Basic Rules VII.A-C, p. 15.

COLLATION (PHYSICAL DESCRIPTION) (Area 5)

Number of globe(s)/relief globe(s): color; diameter in centimeters; types of mounting/other physical characteristics.

A. Number of Items and Specific Designator

1 globe: 1 relief globe:

In simplified cataloging, if the entry describes only one globe, the number and the specific designator "globe" may be omitted since it is the same as the general designator.

E. Color Statement. The abbreviation "col." is used for globes in color. Although some celestial globes may be in black and white or transparent, globes are generally produced in color.

F. Size. Give the diameter in centimeters using the abbreviation "cm."

J. Other Physical Characteristics. A brief description may be given of the type of mounting, surface, meridians, standing height in centimeters, or any other physical properties considered important. When the description cannot be succinctly stated, the information should be given in a note instead of in the Collation.

*The first statement under Imprint, Collation, and Series, shows all the elements in each area as they would be recorded on the catalog card.

plastic markable surface.
semi-meridian.
wood cradle.
40 cm. high.

SERIES (Area 6)

(Series title; number within the series: Subseries title; number within the subseries)

Apply Basic Rules IX.A,B, p. 20.

NOTES (Area 7)

Apply Basic Rules X.A-I, p. 21. Notes are designed to provide supplementary information about the globe not brought out in the formal description. They should be as brief as clarity and good grammar permit, and may be combined and grouped together to create a logical entry.

B. Extension of Physical Description. Give a statement of the scale of the globe (see Card 59). If the scale is not known, the phrase "Scale not given" may be used. For relief globes, the vertical scale, if known, is also given. The scale is transcribed in the units of measure stated on the map, followed, if desired, by the metric conversion in parentheses (see Card 61).

Scale 1:31,680,000.
Scale 1 in.=660 miles (1 cm.=418 km.)
Scale ca. 1: 40,000,000; vertical exaggeration 40:1.

Other pertinent information about the physical properties of the globe are briefly noted. Details of physical description are often combined in the Summary statement.

Wired for internal lighting.
Without geographic grid.
Mounted in fixed semi-meridian on metal base.
Moveable globe pivoted at poles in full meridian circle, in turn pivoted in full horizon circle, pivoted on metal base.

C. Accompanying and/or Descriptive Material. Describe accompanying materials which are designed to assist in the utilization of the globe.

With illustrated handbook. c1974. 8 p.
With 2 audiodiscs: 30 min; 7 in; 33.3 rpm: in illustrated album, 24 p, entitled The story of Mr. World.
With sea and air distance finder.
With a plastic great circle rule, and "Owner's handbook," c1957. 31 p.

E1. Source of Title. Note the source of the title if it is not taken from the globe.

Title from accompanying tag.

H. Summary. The Summary usually provides additional physical description which indicates how information is presented on the globe. The caption "SUMMARY" may be omitted.

OTHER IDENTIFYING AND ORGANIZATIONAL DATA (Area 8)

Apply Basic Rules XI.A-E, p. 24.

D. Media Code. All globes may be coded under the general designator coding for globes "QA", or each format may be coded separately under the coding for its specific designator.

Globe	QF
Relief globe	QR

```
QA
912     Randmark IV globe.  [Globe]  Chicago: Rand
RAN        McNally, c1967.
           1 globe: col; 41 cm; disc-base mounting,
        moveable meridian.  J-H.
           Scale 1 in.:500 miles.
           Wtih globe manual and crayons.
           SUMMARY: A physical-political globe, washable
        surface.  Land elevations, water depths, and
        terrain variations are shown by shades of colors.
        Includes detailed political data.

        GLOBES                  O
```

CARD 59
Globe.
Title main entry.
General medium code in call number.
Educational level note.

```
QR
912     Nystrom raised relief globe.  [Globe]  Chicago:
NYS        Nystrom, [196-]
           1 relief globe: col; 31 cm; gyro-disc mount-
        ing.
           With distance finder.
           A physical-political globe, markable plastic
        surface.



        GLOBES
```

CARD 60
Relief globe.
Title main entry.
Specific medium code in call number.

```
912     Hydrographic relief globe.  [Globe]  Northbrook,
HYD        IL: Hubbard, c1962.
           1 relief globe: col; 31 cm; plastic, in plas-
        tic cradle.
           Scale 1:41,817,600; 1 in.=660 miles (1 cm.=
        418 km); vertical exaggeration 40:1.
           Without geographic grid.
           With illustrated handbook.
           Raised surfaces show land contours and the
        Equator.  Ocean surfaces are in clear plastic
        through which the topography of the ocean floor
        may be seen.
        GLOBES/ OCEAN
                                            QA:QR
```

CARD 61
Relief globe.
Title main entry.
Medium code at bottom of card.
Metric conversion.

523.402 Planetary celestial globe. [Globe] Developed
PLA by Herbert R. Baerg at the Jet Propulsion
Laboratory for NASA. Hubbard, [197-]
1 globe: col; 31 cm; transparent.
With study guide.
A model of the planet orbits is mounted inside the globe so that the positions of Mercury, Mars, Venus, and Earth may be plotted without using planetary tables. The Earth model may be positioned from outside the sphere.

GLOBES, CELESTIAL/ PLANETS/ Baerg, Herbert R.

CARD 62
Globe.
Title main entry.
Statement of creator responsibility.
Place omitted.

Medium Designator: **KIT**

Specific Designators:
Exhibit
Kit
Laboratory kit
Programed instruction kit

Description

A *kit* is a collection of materials, in one or more than one medium, that are subject related and intended for use as a unit. In a package that contains more than one medium, often called a multimedia kit, no one medium is so clearly dominant that the others are dependent or accompanying. The *principal* components of a multimedia kit may be of sufficient significance that, if desired, they can be entered in the catalog as analytics or as separately cataloged entities. A filmstrip with a synchronized audiorecording and an accompanying teacher's guide with script, though issued as a unit, is not cataloged as a kit but as a filmstrip, which is the dominant medium. Such a unit, however, may be included as part of a kit containing related material in other media formats. The materials in a kit in only one medium are specifically designed and coordinated to be used according to a prescribed method, as in *a programed instruction kit* that leads the user through sequential steps to an understanding of the subject; or for a particular purpose, as in a *laboratory kit.*

MAIN ENTRY (Area 1)

Apply Basic Rules IV.A-C, p. 4.

A. Title Main Entry. Title main entry is preferred since kits are usually identified by title by the producer and the user.

B. Series Title Main Entry. When kits are issued in a series, main entry under series title may be made in accordance with Basic Rules IV.B1-3 (see Card 66).

C. Creator Main Entry. A kit may be entered under the name of the creator if the overall responsibility for the intellectual and artistic content can be attributed to one person or corporate body, and *if the name is significant in identifying the work.* An added entry is made for the title (see Card 64).

Creator main entry may occur more frequently for programed instruction kits which contain only texts and instructions whose authorship is clearly indicated.

TITLE/MEDIUM DESIGNATOR/STATEMENT OF CREATOR RESPONSIBILITY (Area 2)

A. Title. Apply Basic Rules V.A1-10, p. 7. The title of the kit is taken from the container in which the various materials are packaged. Varying titles which appear conspicuously on different pieces within the kit may be ignored unless the entire kit is likely to be identified by these titles. In such cases, the variant titles may be cited in a note. Added entries may be made if desired, but are usually not necessary.

B. Medium Designator. Apply Basic Rule V.B1, p. 10. The general physical form designator (medium designator) "Kit" is given in the singular form following the Title statement and is usually enclosed in square brackets. The brackets may be omitted (see Card 68).

C. Statement of Creator Responsibility. Apply Basic Rule V.C, p. 13 (see Cards 64, 67).

EDITION (Area 3)

Apply Basic Rule VI, p. 14. (see Card 67).

IMPRINT (Area 4)*

Place: Producer, copyright/production date; sponsored by Sponsor; Place: Distributed/Released by Distributor, release date.

Apply Basic Rules VII.A-C, p. 15.

COLLATION (PHYSICAL DESCRIPTION) (Area 5)

Number of exhibit(s)/kit(s)/laboratory kit(s)/programed instruction kit(s): description of parts; description of container, height × width × depth in centimeters.

A. Number of Items and Specific Designator

1 exhibit: 1 kit: 4 laboratory kits:
1 programed instruction kit:

*The first statement under Imprint, Collation, and Series, shows all the elements in each area as they would be recorded on the catalog card.

The inclusion of more than one kit in a catalog entry seldom occurs. If one entry is made for an entire program that consists of several parts, each of which is a complete kit, the total number of kits would be given, e.g., 4 programed instruction kits. It is recommended, however, that each part (kit) be cataloged as a separate entry since many resource centers may not acquire all the kits in the program.

In simplified cataloging, when the entry is for one kit, the number of items and the specific designator, which is the same as the general designator, may be omitted.

B. Physical Contents. List the types of material in the kit, and their number if it is easily ascertainable. No order of listing can be prescribed because of the wide variety in kit components. In general, if the kit contains an inventory, the items are transcribed as listed. Otherwise, they are recorded alphabetically.

If a physical description of the component media is considered necessary, it may be included in the Collation area when it can be succinctly stated. Otherwise, the information is given in the Notes area. In some instances, instead of making a distinction between the Collation and Notes areas, the contents of a kit may be more briefly and logically described by disregarding the prescribed areas of recording information and combining the required physical and bibliographic details in a continuous statement (see Card 65).

J. Other Physical Characteristics. Give a brief description and the dimensions (height × width × depth in centimeters) of the container.

in wicker carrying case.
in box, 18 × 25 × 19 cm.

SERIES (Area 6)

(Series title; number within the series: Subseries title; number within the subseries)

Apply Basic Rules IX.A,B, p. 20.

NOTES (Area 7)

Apply Basic Rules X.A-I, p. 21. Notes are designed to provide supplementary information about the kit not brought out in the formal description. They should be as brief as clarity and good grammar permit, and may be combined and grouped together to create a logical entry. In some instances, Collation and Notes are combined to convey a clearer image of the work (see Physical Contents). The fullness of detail in notes will vary according to the needs of the particular clientele.

A. Educational Level. If desired, the educational level for which the kit is intended may be noted following the Series statement. The terms or abbreviations given in Basic Rule X.A are used (see Card 64). Or, the educational level, audience suitability and/or restrictions may be described in the Summary.

B. Extension of Physical Description. Give additional information required for the physical description, the equipment, or other materials needed to fully utilize the work.

Inventory and student instructions on inside of container lid.
Use with the Mast Teaching Machine.

C. Accompanying and/or Descriptive Material. Teacher's guides, student manuals, and other similar descriptive and instructional materials are usually part of the contents of the kit and are recorded in the physical description (see Collation). When packaged separately, such material or equipment, is considered accompanying material and is described in a note.

H. Summary. The intent of the kit should be stated. The grade level may be included in the Summary if it has not been given in the Educational level note. For programed instruction give the basic program type (linear, branching, mixed construction), response mode (written, spoken), and any other pertinent information that will help the searcher understand how the program functions.

I. Contents. Titles of components that are distinctive and descriptive of the subject content of the kit may be given in a Contents or Partial Contents note. Titles of components are often combined with information in the Collation (see Cards 63, 65). The caption "CONTENTS" or "PARTIAL CONTENTS" may be omitted.

OTHER IDENTIFYING AND ORGANIZATIONAL DATA (Area 8)

Apply Basic Rules XI.A-E, p. 24.

D. Media Code. The several formats of kits may be coded together under the general designator coding for kits "KA", or each format may be coded separately under the coding for its specific designator.

Exhibit	KE
Kit	KT
Laboratory kit	KL
Programed instruction kit	KP

```
KA
701     Art and war.  [Kit]  Englewood Cliffs, NJ:
ART        Scholastic Book Services, c1971.
           1 kit: teaching guide; Art & man magazine,
        Mar. 1971, 31 copies; set of 16 slides, col, en-
        titled Men in battle, ancient times to 20th cen-
        tury; portfolio of facsimile reproductions of
        Goya's etchings.  (Art & man units, 1970-71)
           SUMMARY: Surveys how war has been presented
        in art.

        ART AND WAR/ WAR/ ser
```

CARD 63
Kit.
Title main entry.
General medium code in call number.

```
KT
372.6   Urban, Alex
URB        On stage: Wally, Bertha, and you.  [Kit]
        Created by Alex Urban.  Chicago: Encyclopaedia
        Britannica Educational Corp., c1971.
           1 kit: activity, story, picture, and construc-
        tion cards; 2 hand puppets; teacher's guide.  P.
           SUMMARY: Creative and dramatic activities
        designed to give children experience in oral
        expression and communication skills.
        COMMUNICATION/ ENGLISH LANGUAGE- STUDY AND
        TEACHING/ t
```

CARD 64
Kit.
Creator main entry.
Specific medium code in call number.
Statement of creator responsibility.
Educational level note.

301.45 Negro history. [Kit] Chicago: Society for
NEG Visual Education, c1964.
1 kit: book entitled Great Negroes, past and present, by Russell L. Adams; 48 mounted pictures in 2 portfolios; 6 transparencies, with guide; 6 filmstrips: 43-48 fr, col. & 3 audiodiscs, with 6 teacher's guides, entitled Mary McLeod Bethune, George Washington Carver, Benjamin Banneker, Robert Smalls, Frederick Douglass, Harriet Tubman.
NEGROES- BIOGRAPHY/ NEGROES- HISTORY

CARD 65
Kit.
Title main entry.
Collation and notes combined.

560 Fossils - the record of life. [Kit] North-
FOS brook, IL: Hubbard, [196-]
5 laboratory kits: 20 reproduction fossils each; 5 student laboratory manuals.
SUMMARY: Each kit contains fossils selected to provide a number of different investigations involving stratigraphic correlation, geologic history and mapping, and environmental study.

FOSSILS/ GEOLOGY

KA:KL

CARD 66
Laboratory kit set.
Set title main entry.
Medium code at bottom of card.

```
428.4    Reading laboratory IIIa, grades 7-9.  [Kit]
REA-3a      Developed by Don H. Parker.  Rev. ed.
1973        Chicago: Science Research Associates, c1973.
            1 programed instruction kit: teacher's hand-
         book; 10 sets of Power builders with key cards;
         10 sets of Rate builders with key booklets;
         student record book; colored pencils.
            SUMMARY: An individualized learning program
         for reading improvement.  Components are ar-
         ranged in order of difficulty and color-keyed.
         READING/ Parker, Don H./ Science Research
         Associates
```

CARD 67
Programed instruction kit.
Title main entry.
Statement of creator responsibility.
Edition statement.
Producer added entry.

```
428.4    Reading laboratory IIIa, grades 7-9.  Kit.
REA-3a      Rev. ed.  SRA, c1973.
1973        1 programed instruction kit: teacher's hand-
         book; various color-keyed cards and booklets.
            An individualized program for reading im-
         provement.



         READING/ Science Research Associates
```

CARD 68
Programed instruction kit.
Title main entry.
Simplified cataloging.

Medium Designator: **MACHINE-READABLE DATA FILE**

Specific Designators:
- Species of file:
  - Data file
  - Program file
- Storage medium:
  - Disc
  - Punched card
  - Punched paper tape
  - Tape

Description

A machine-readable data file (MRDF) is a collection of related records that are treated as a unit and represented in such a way that they can be read and/or translated by a machine. The file may reside on a variety of different storage media including discs, punched cards, magnetic tapes, etc. The physical description of an MRDF should not be definitive since the information stored on one medium can be transferred easily to another, e.g., punched cards to magnetic tapes.

Specific Designators

Since the storage medium of a machine-readable data file can be changed as required, the specific designator, for purposes of the catalog record, indicates the species of file rather than the medium which carries the data. A *data file* includes all the facts, numbers, letters, and symbols that refer to or describe an object, idea, condition, situation, etc. A descriptor such as a survey file, an historical file, or a textual file, is often used to indicate more precisely the nature of the data contained in a file. The terms "data file" and "data set" are often used interchangeably even though the definition for "data set" may vary according to computer languages and individual usage. A *program file* contains the instructions which control the operation of the computer so that it performs the tasks required to produce the desired result.

Specific designators which indicate the physical properties of data file storage are usually not included in the permanent catalog record since users of data files are not involved in manipulating the files, and the storage medium may not remain the same. A record of the current physical status of files is usually kept in the computer center for the information of the center's personnel. However, if a local facility wishes to include the physical designator in the public catalog, specific designators for some of the most commonly used storage media have been provided. Specific designators for other types of stores such as drums, magnetic cards, magnetic ink or optical character recognition documents, etc., may be assigned by the cataloger should the need arise. If the specific designators "disc" and "tape" are used out of context with the general designator "Machine-readable data file", it is recommended that they be combined with the descriptor "digital" (e.g., digital disc, digital tape) to avoid a possible ambiguity in medium.

MAIN ENTRY (Area 1)

Machine-readable data files usually contain alphanumeric data and are therefore, in general, entered in accordance with the rules for main entry for books and book-like materials in Part I of the *Anglo-American Cataloging Rules*. However, if the contents are essentially representations that are characteristic of a work in an audiovisual medium, the MRDF is entered in accordance with Basic Rules IV.A-C, p. 4, as applied to the particular type of material (q.v.). If a work originally produced in another medium is stored in a machine-readable data file, the file is entered in the same manner as the original work.

A. Title Main Entry. If intellectual responsibility is diffuse or in doubt, a machine-readable data file is entered under an established title. (See Title/Medium Designator/Statement of Creator Responsibility, (Area 2); Notes, (Area 7); Title; and Card 71.)

B. Series Title Main Entry. A machine-readable data file is entered under a serial, series, or set title in accordance with the rules in Part I, AACR, and Basic Rules IV.B1-3, p. 5, (see Card 74).

C. Creator Main Entry. Since the intellectual responsibility for the information stored in a machine-readable data file can usually be attributed to a person or corporate body, a MRDF is generally entered under the name of the creator, in accordance with the rules for author entry in Part I, *AACR* (see Cards 69, 72, 73).

TITLE/MEDIUM DESIGNATOR/STATEMENT OF CREATOR RESPONSIBILITY (Area 2)

A. Title. Apply Basic Rules V.A1-10, p. 7. The title is taken from an internal user label or its substitute preceding or within the machine-readable data file itself, or from an equivalent such as a printout or cathode ray tube image. Labeling standards, however, are still in the process of being finalized, and many files may have no interior label or internal statement of the title or the bibliographic information needed for cataloging. The title, as well as details concerning the creator, imprint, and other essential elements must therefore be obtained from accompanying documentation prepared by the producer, distributor, creator, editor, etc., and/or from other external sources such as published descriptions in articles, reference works, distributors' brochures, etc. Such sources of information for the title and any of the elements should be given in a note (see Source of Title, pp. 22, 124, and Cards 69, 70, 72, 74). A machine-readable data file container is not an integral part of the data stored within it and is generally disregarded as a source of any cataloging information.

A machine-readable data file may frequently be named by a variety of titles. In selecting a title, the cataloger should be guided by the purpose of the work, and the prevalence of citation in use and in reference sources. Acronymic titles, which are often more familiar to the user than the fuller titles which they abridge, may be used. Variant titles and the full title for an acronym may be given in a note and added entries may be made for them as considered necessary. Data set names, which are locally and arbitrarily assigned and which may often be unrelated to the files' contents, are not considered valid identifiers and should be avoided. If no suitable title is found, one which is descriptive of the nature and scope of the contents of the file may be supplied by the cataloger and enclosed in brackets. The source of information upon which the composed title is based may be given in a note (see Source of Title, pp. 22, 124).

The notation of the volumes and the period covered in closed and open serial files is included in the title statement (see Cards 71, 74).

B. Medium Designator. Apply Basic Rule V.B1, p. 10. The general physical form designator (medium designator) "Machine-readable data file" is given in a singular form following the Title statement and is usually enclosed in square brackets. The brackets may be omitted. If it will be understood by the user, the abbreviation "MRDF" may be substituted for the medium designator spelled out in full (see Card 71).

C. Statement of Creator Responsibility. Apply Basic Rule V.C, p. 13. Creator responsibility is given when the functions performed can be definitely assigned and briefly stated. The statement is often omitted, however, since the nature of machine-readable data files makes it extremely difficult to identify exactly the type of work done by a person or corporate body in the creation of the file. While the intellectual responsibility for the actual information input may often be attributed to the person or corporate body chosen for the main entry, the creation of the file itself necessitates the preparation of data for conversion to machine-readable form. The process of compiling, editing, and manipulating data demands a considerable intellectual contribution that may be made by one or several persons. If considered pertinent, a note concerning those involved in data preparation may be given.

EDITION (Area 3)

Apply Basic Rule VI, p. 14. Since machine-readable data files are often subject to change, a file in which data has been deleted or added may not be considered a new or revised edition. Information should be given in a note or in the Summary regarding the frequency of issue, the updating of data, and the significance of dates, all of which may assist the potential user in making a decision about the relevance of the file for his needs.

IMPRINT (Area 4)*

Place: Producer, production date; sponsored by Sponsor; Place: Distributed/Released by Distributor, release date.

A. Place. Apply Basic Rule VII.A, p. 15. When several organizations are involved in the production and release of the file, give the location of each of the organizations. Place may be omitted (see Cards 69-71) except for machine-readable data files that are not commercially produced.

B. Producer/ Sponsor/ Distributor. Apply Basic Rules VII.B1-4, p. 16. The processing and releasing of a machine-readable data file may be the work of persons and organizations other than those usually accepted as producers, sponsors, and distributors. When applicable, copyright owners, computer centers, project groups, and others who participated in the work of production may be given as producers. In some instances, several names may have to be recorded. The phrase "Distributed by" or "Released by" which indicates the function of the distributor may be omitted, if desired.

C. Date. Give the date the file was produced, and if different, the original release date. An approximate date may have to be supplied. Sources from which the approximation is derived, such as dates of supplementary files and time periods of data collection, are given in a note.

COLLATION (PHYSICAL DESCRIPTION) (Area 5)

Number of data file(s)/program file(s): number of logical records/ number and language of program statements; other physical characteristics.

A. Number of Items and Specific Designator

1. *Species of file specific designator.* Give the number of files and the species of file specific designator.

1 data file: 3 data files: 1 program file:

In recording the number of files, care should be taken to distinguish between a single file that is stored in more than one physical entity

*The first statement under Imprint, Collation, and Series, shows all the elements in each area as they would be recorded on the catalog card.

(i.e., disc, tape, etc.), which should be designated as 1 data file, and a multi-file which contains several files that are essentially parts of a work cataloged under one title. Since each part of a multi-file entry is a complete file in itself that could be cataloged as a separate entry, the total number of files included in the multi-file entry is given (see Cards 72, 73).

2. *Storage medium specific designator.* Since machine-readable data may often be transferred from one storage medium to another, the physical description of the type of material on which the data is recorded is usually not given. However, if a physical description of the store on the catalog record (see Card 71) is deemed necessary by the particular facility, information such as the following may be given as required:

a. Number of physical entities

b. Storage medium specific designator

c. The particular type of material and, as appropriate, its size, quantitative properties, trade name, etc.

1 data file: 1 disc, diameter of disc;
1 tape, reel, diameter of reel, length/width of tape, number of channels, e.g., 7 channel, 9 channel;
1 tape, cassette, dimensions of cassette;
2 tapes, cartridge, dimensions of cartridge;
150 punched cards, number of columns (e.g., 80 columns, 90 columns), type of card (e.g., Stub, IBM System 3);

When the storage medium specific designators "disc" and "tape" are not used in context with their species of file specific designators or general designator, to avoid an ambiguity in medium they are preceded by the descriptor "digital", i.e., digital disc, digital tape.

F. Size of File. The size of a data file is recorded as the number of logical records. A *logical record* is a single unit of information consisting of one or more fields of variables. If the size of the file has not been verified by machine count, this fact is given in a note (see Extension of Physical Description, and Cards 69, 70).

For *program files,* the number of program statements and the language of the program is given.

1 program file: 100 Cobol statements;

If the entry describes one machine-readable data file stored in more than one physical volume (discs, tapes, etc.), the total number of logical records included in all the volumes is given.

1 data file: 2 tapes, reel, 12 in; 13000 logical records;

If the entry describes more than one machine-readable data file, the number of logical records in each file is given (see Card 72). The number of logical records may be omitted from the Collation and recorded after the title of each file in the Contents note (see Card 73).

J. Other Physical Characteristics. Additional descriptive details such as labeling information, may be included in the Collation if they can be briefly stated.

1 data file: 1500 logical records; standard label.

Longer statements such as descriptions of logical records, are given in a note (see Extension of Physical Description, and Cards 72, 73).

When the specific storage medium designator is recorded in the Collation, additional physical properties of the store may be described. Such pertinent details may include the code, e.g., BCD (Binary Coded Decimal), Hexadecimal, etc., the number of characters per record, the density, e.g., number of bpi (bits per inch) or cpi (characters per inch), odd or even parity, etc., as pertinent (see Card 71). In some instances, when these physical characteristics are given, the number of logical records is omitted.

SERIES (Area 6)

(Series title; number within the series: Subseries title; number within the subseries)

Apply Basic Rules IX.A,B, p. 20.

NOTES (Area 7)

Apply Basic Rules X.A-I, p. 21. Notes are designed to provide supplementary information about the machine-readable data file not brought out in the formal description. They should be as brief as clarity and good grammar permit, and may be combined or grouped together to create a clear informational and descriptive statement.

B. Extension of Physical Description. Give information concerning verification of file size (see Cards 69, 70) and descriptions of logical records (see Cards 72, 73) and other physical characteristics considered pertinent.

C. Accompanying and/or Descriptive Material. Note the existence of a separate code book or other supplementary documentation provided with the file. Such accompanying material is often the source for bibliographic, physical, and content information. The notation may be a simple statement that indicates the purpose of the accompanying material, e.g., With format; With code book (see Cards 69-71), or it may include identifying bibliographic details and pagination.

E1. Source of Title. When an internal statement or its equivalent does not provide a title, note the external source from which the title is taken (see Cards 69, 70, 72, 74). When a title is composed by the cataloger, the source of information upon which the composition is based is given.

Title based on print-out.
Title derived from verbal description of depositor.

E2. Title Variations. Note variant titles, acronymic and catchword titles or such titles spelled out in full, and other titles under which the work may be known (see Cards 69, 70), and make added entries for them as necessary. For data set names, notation and added entries are optional.

H. Summary. A summary is essential for machine-readable data files. In addition to the content summary, the note may include source of date(s), physical characteristics, restrictions on use, condition of the file, and explanations deemed necessary for clarification of information given in the entry, or for guidance in methods of using the file. The caption "SUMMARY" may be omitted.

I. Contents. A listing of separate content items in machine-readable data files is usually impractical. However, when the entry is a multi-file entity, the title of each file is recorded in the Contents note. The number of logical records in each file is noted after its title if the size of the file has not been given in the Collation (see Card 73). The caption "CONTENTS" may be omitted.

OTHER IDENTIFYING AND ORGANIZATIONAL DATA (Area 8)

Apply Basic Rules XI.A-E, p. 24.

D. Media Code. All machine-readable data files may be coded under the general designator coding for machine-readable data files "DA", or each species of file may be coded separately under the coding for its specific designator. If a facility requires coding for the file's physical store, the MDRF may be coded under the coding for its storage medium specific designator.

Species of file	Data file	DF
	Program file	DE
Storage medium	Disc	DD
	Punched card	DB
	Punched paper tape	DP
	Tape	DT

```
DA
309.173 Davis, James Allen
DAV        National data program for the social sciences:
        Spring, 1972 general social survey.  [Machine-
        readable data file]  Chicago: National Opinion
        Research Center; Roper Public Opinion Research
        Center, 1972.
           1 data file: 1613 logical records.
           Size of file not verified.
           With code book.
           Title from code book.  Also known as 1972
        NORC general social survey.

                                  (See next card)
```

CARD 69
Machine-readable data file.
Creator main entry.
General medium code in call number.
Notes:
Extension of physical description.
Accompanying material.
Title source and variants.
Summary.
Place of Distributor omitted.

```
                                          (Card 2)
DA
309.173 Davis, James Allen
DAV        National data program for the social sciences.
        Spring, 1972 general social survey.  [Machine-
        readable data file]

           SUMMARY: Opinions on social stratification,
        family, race relations, social control, civil
        liberties, and morale; compiled from the res-
        ponses of 1613 adults to 61 questions.

        SOCIAL SURVEYS- U.S./ U.S.- SOCIAL CONDITIONS/
        t: 1972 NORC gen    eral social survey./ t
```

CARD 69A
Continuation card.

```
DA
309.173 Davis, James Allen.
DAV        National data program for the social sciences,
        Spring, 1972 general social survey / [Machine-
        readable data file]. - Chicago : National Opinion
        Research Center ; Roper Public Opinion Research
        Center, 1972.
           1 data file : 1613 logical records.
           Size of file not verified.
           With code book.
           Title from code book.  Also known as 1972
        NORC general social survey.

                                   (See next card)
```

CARD 70
Machine-readable data file.
Creator main entry.
ISBD punctuation
(Card 1 shown only).

```
DF
330.973 U.S. economic data tape.  2477 series.  [MRDF]
UNI        Brookings Institution, 1970.
           1 data file: 1 tape, reel, 12 in.(31 cm.); 7
        tracks; blocked BCD's; 49 records per block; 90
        characters per record; 800 bpi; odd parity;
        standard label.
           With format.
           Covers data relating to the period 1947-1965,
        obtained from a survey of current business, the
        Bureau of Labor Statistics, a Federal Reserve
        bulletin, and the Securities and Exchange Com-
        mission.
        ECONOMICS- STATISTICS/ U.S.- ECONOMIC CON-
        DITIONS
```

CARD 71
Machine-readable data file.
Title main entry.
Specific medium code in call number.
Series number included in title.
General medium designator abbreviated.
Place omitted.
Storage medium in Collation.
Summary (caption omitted).

```
317.3   U. S.  Bureau of the Census
UNI        1970 censuses of population and housing,
        fifth count summary tape, sample.  [Machine-
        readable data file]  Rosslyn, VA: DUALabs, 1973.
           2 data files: 1000, 12000 logical records.
           Each logical record made up of 4 physical
        records of 1920 characters.
           Title from DUALabs Technical document ST-5.
           CONTENTS: File A.  Summaries for 3 digit ZIP
        code areas.- File B.  Summaries for 5 digit ZIP
        code areas completely within Standard Metropoli-
        tan Statistical        Areas.
        U.S.- CENSUS
                                            DA:DF
```

CARD 72
Machine-readable data file: multi-file.
Creator (body) main entry.
Size of files in Collation.
Medium code at bottom of card.

```
317.3   U. S.  Bureau of the Census
UNI        1970 censuses of population and housing,
        fifth count summary tape, sample.  [Machine-
        readable data file]  Rosslyn, VA: DUALabs, 1973.
           2 data files.
           Each logical record made up of 4 physical
        records of 1920 characters.
           File A.  Summaries for 3 digit ZIP code areas,
        1000 logical records.- File B.  Summaries for 5
        digit ZIP code areas completely within Standard
        Metropolitan Statistical Areas, 12000 logical
        records.

        U.S.- CENSUS
```

CARD 73
Machine-readable data file: multi-file.
Creator (body) main entry.
Size of files in Contents note.
Contents (caption omitted).

540.05 CA condensates. Vol. 69- . July 1968-
CHE [Machine-readable data file] Columbus, OH:
Chemical Abstracts Service, 1968-
data files.

Title from Chemical Abstracts Service specifications manual.

Updated weekly, indexing Chemical Abstracts sections 1-34 and 35-80 in alternating weeks corresponding to CA issues.

CHEMISTRY- PERIODICALS- INDEXES/ Chemical Abstracts.

CARD 74
Machine-readable data file.
Serial title main entry.
Open entry.

Medium Designator: **MAP**

Specific Designators:
Map
Relief map
Wall map

Description

A *map* is a representation, usually on a flat surface, of areas of the earth (terrestrial map) or of the heavens (celestial map). A *relief map* shows contours in raised surfaces.

Maps are issued singly and in sets. Those that are of temporary value because of poor durability or continuously changing data should be treated as vertical file material.

MAIN ENTRY (Area 1)

Apply Basic Rules IV.A-C, p. 4.

A. Title Main Entry. Title entry is usually preferred for maps. The name of the producer may often occur as the initial word in the title.

B. Series Title Main Entry. When maps are issued in a set or series, each map is generally cataloged under its own title. However, maps in a set or series that present different aspects or parts of an area or subject are entered as a unit under the series title (see Card 76). When an individual map in the set is cataloged as a separate entity, its title is treated as a subtitle of the set title (see Card 79).

C. Creator Main Entry. Main entry may be made under the cartographer's name *if it is significant in identifying the map.* Commercial firms that produce maps are not considered for main entry. The producer's name may, however, appear as the initial word in a title main entry.

TITLE/MEDIUM DESIGNATOR/STATEMENT OF CREATOR RESPONSIBILITY (Area 2)

A. Title. Apply Basic Rules VA.1-10, p. 7. The title is taken from any part of the face of the map, preference being given to a title within the border. If there is no title, or the words of the title are scattered so that the order is not obvious, the title is taken from accompanying data or the producer's catalog. If no title is found in the reference sources, the name of the area or subject covered is supplied as the title by the cataloger and shown in brackets. The area name selected should be taken from an authoritative list such as *Webster's Geographical Dictionary*. For large collections, *Gazetteers*, from the U.S.

Board on Geographic Names, and *Geographic Bulletins* issued by the Office of the Geographer, U.S. Dept. of State, provide more detailed information.

Titles of insets and marginal material are given in notes (see Accompanying and/or Descriptive Material, pp. 22, 132).

B. Medium Designator. Apply Basic Rule V.B1, p. 10. The general physical form designator (medium designator) "Map" is given in the singular form following the Title statement and is usually enclosed in square brackets. The brackets may be omitted.

C. Statement of Creator Responsibility. Apply Basic Rule V.C, p. 13. The name(s) of the cartographer(s), editor(s) and/or other person(s) responsible for researching the data needed to create the map may be stated after the medium designator *if they are significant in identifying the work*, and added entries may be made for them, as considered necessary (see Card 77).

EDITION (Area 3)

Apply Basic Rule VI, p. 14.

IMPRINT (Area 4)*

Place: Producer, copyright/production date; sponsored by Sponsor; Place: Distributed/Released by Distributor, release date.

Apply Basic Rules VII.A-C, p. 15.

COLLATION (PHYSICAL DESCRIPTION) (Area 5)

Number of map(s)/relief map(s)/wall map(s): color/black and white; height × width in centimeters; mount/other physical characteristics.

A. Number of Items and Specific Designator

1 map: 10 maps: 1 relief map: 1 wall map:

The number recorded is the number of sheets. When more than one map is printed on one sheet, this information is given in the Extension of physical description or in the Summary note. In simplified cataloging, if the entry describes only one map, the number and the specific designator "map" may be omitted since it is the same as the general designator.

*The first statement under Imprint, Collation, and Series, shows all the elements in each area as they would be recorded on the catalog card.

When a map qualifies for more than one specific designator, e.g., a relief map that is also a wall map, the specific designator should be selected that describes the physical characteristic judged to be the most meaningful for concept content. The other physical characteristic is described in a note (see Card 78).

E. Color Statement. The abbreviation "col." is used for maps in color, "b&w" for those in black and white. Maps except outline maps, are usually colored.

F. Size. Give the height × the width of the entire sheet on which the map is printed in centimeters. If the border dimensions of the map(s) are considered important, they are given in a note (see Card 75).

J. Other Physical Characteristics. A brief description may be given of the mount, surface, material from which the map is made, or any other physical properties considered important. When the description cannot be succinctly stated, the information should be given in a note instead of in the Collation.

laminated.
markable surface.
clothbacked.
heavy paper folded to 11 × 8½ in. (28 × 22 cm.)
mounted on spring roller.

SERIES (Area 6)

(Series title; number within the series: Subseries title; number within the subseries)

Apply Basic Rules IX.A,B, p. 20.

NOTES (Area 7)

Apply Basic Rules X.A-I, p. 21. Notes are designed to provide supplementary information about the map not brought out in the formal description. They should be as brief as clarity and good grammar permit, and may be combined and grouped together to create a logical entry.

B. Extension of Physical Description. Give a statement of the scale of the map, if known. The scale is omitted if it cannot be easily ascertained, or the phrase "Scale not given" may be used. For relief maps, the vertical scale, if known, is also given. The scale is transcribed in the units of measure stated on the map, followed, if desired, by the metric conversion in parentheses.

Scale 9 inches=24 miles (1 cm.=1.69 km.)
Scale 1 in.:169 miles; vertical exaggeration 15:1.
Scale in latitude 71°=1:3,000,000; vertical exaggeration 30 times.

Other pertinent information such as map projection, topographical features, etc., are briefly noted. Details of physical description are often combined in the Summary statement.

Bonne's projection.
Azimuthal equidistant projection.
Elevations shown by layer tints.
Relief indicated by form lines.

C. Accompanying and/or Descriptive Material. Information printed on the sheet, such as margin notes, indexes, insets, and other maps, are described, as well as accompanying materials designed to assist in the utilization of the map (see Cards 75, 76, 79).

Issued with the National geographic magazine, May 1970.
Key to place names in margin.
3 insets: Australia, Tasmania, New Zealand.
Street index on verso.
Maps of Alaska and Hawaii on verso.
2 maps printed on each side.

H. Summary. The Summary usually includes a statement of any special purpose for which the map is designed, and additional physical description. The caption "SUMMARY" may be omitted (see Cards 76-79).

OTHER IDENTIFYING AND ORGANIZATIONAL DATA (Area 8)

Apply Basic Rules XI.A-E, p. 24.

D. Media Code. All maps may be coded under the general designator coding for maps "LA", or each format may be coded separately under the coding for its specific designator.

Map	LM
Relief map	LR
Wall map	LW

```
LA
917.44  South Hadley.  [Map]  Chicago: Rand McNally,
SOU        c1969.
           1 map: col; 40 x 60 cm.
           Scale 1 inch=4 miles.
           Size of map, 9 x 20 cm.
           Street index in margins.
           Title on outside when folded: New map of
        South Hadley and vicinity.

        SOUTH HADLEY, MA- MAPS/ t: New map of South
        Hadley and vicinity.
```

CARD 75
Map.
Title main entry.
General medium code in call number.
Notes:
Extension of physical description. Accompanying and/or descriptive materials. Title.

```
LW
917.3   Visual-history wall maps.  [Map]  Washington,
VIS        DC: Civic Education Service, [196-?]
           10 wall maps: col; 64 x 92 cm.  I-H.
           With teacher's guide; historical notes inset.
           SUMMARY: Each map highlights key aspects in
        America's history.
           CONTENTS: Exploration.- Colonization.- Ameri-
        can Revolution.- Western frontier.- American In-
        dians.- Immigration.- House divided.- Civil War.-
        Literary America.- 20th century America.
        U.S.- HISTORICAL GEOGRAPHY- MAPS
```

CARD 76
Wall map set.
Set title main entry.
Specific medium code in call number.
Notes:
Educational level. Accompanying and/or descriptive materials. Summary. Contents.

```
915.2   Japan.  [Map]  Ed. by Norton S. Ginsburg.
JAP        Chicago: Denoyer-Geppert, c1972.
           1 wall map: col; 112 x 148 cm; clothbacked,
        mounted on spring roller.
           Scale 9 in.:24 miles.
           A physical-political map that shows express-
        ways, densely inhabited districts, and railroad
        patterns.

        JAPAN- MAPS/ Ginsburg, Norton S.
```

CARD 77
Wall map.
Title main entry.
Statement of creator responsibility; added entry for name cited.
Summary (caption omitted).

```
912     Asia.  [Map]  Nystrom, c1971.
ASI        1 relief map: col; 107 x 122 cm; laminated.
           Scale 1 in.:169 miles; vertical exaggeration
        15:1.
           A wall map which shows all of Asia and Europe,
        parts of Africa and Australia, ocean depths,
        and elevations.

        ASIA- MAPS/ EUROPE- MAPS
```

LA:LR

CARD 78
Relief map.
Title main entry.
Place omitted.
Medium code at bottom of card.

550.9 Geologic map portfolio. No. 2, Historical geo-
GEO-2 logy. [Map] Rochester, NJ: Ward's Natural Science Establishment, [196-]
13 maps: col; 54 x 36 cm.
With 13 incomplete corresponding structure sections, text, and student exercises.
Illustrates surface and subsurface rocks found in the major geologic provinces of the U.S.

GEOLOGY- MAPS/ ROCKS/ t: Historical geology.

CARD 79
One set of maps from a series.
Series title main entry.

Medium Designator: **MICROFORM**

Specific Designators:
- Aperture card
- Card
- Cartridge
- Cassette
- Fiche
- Reel
- Ultrafiche

Description

A *microform* is a reproduction, greatly reduced in size, of alphanumeric or graphic matter. To be read, a microform must be magnified. Microforms may be either opaque or transparent. Opaque microforms contain images printed on sheets of opaque material and require a reading device that employs reflected light and magnifies the images. An opaque microform printed on card stock is designated as a *card*. Microcard and microprint are registered trademarks for card microforms which differ in size, reduction ratio, and reading equipment requirements. A 3 × 5 inch (8 × 13 cm.) Microcard can reproduce up to 48 pages; a 6 × 9 inch (15 × 23 cm.) Microprint up to 106 pages.

Transparent microforms contain images on translucent material and require a reading device that employs transmitted light and magnifies the images. A transparent microform photographed on film (i.e., microfilm) may be produced in different sizes, reduction ratios, and formats, each of which may necessitate special reading equipment. In a *cartridge* the ends of the enclosed microfilm are spliced together to form a continuous loop; in a *cassette* the enclosed microfilm winds and rewinds from reel to reel. A *reel* is a roll of microfilm on an open reel. Cartridge, cassette, and reel microfilms are usually 35mm or 16mm in width. A roll of 35mm microfilm can reproduce up to 1000 pages. Short lengths of 16 or 35mm microfilm may be stored in the pockets of a transparent plastic carrier called a jacket. Microfilm in a jacket is usually treated as vertical file material since it may often be replaced by strips that bear updated data.

An *aperture card* is a data card with a 16mm, 35mm, or 70mm microfilm insert. A *fiche* is a sheet of film, usually 4 × 6 inches (105 × 148 mm.) containing multiple images in a grid pattern. Pages have been reduced sufficiently (i.e., up to 90×) to reproduce up to 208 pages per sheet. An *ultrafiche* is a sheet of film, usually 4 × 6 inches (105 × 148 mm.) with an image reduction greater than that of a fiche (i.e., above 90×) that permits reproduction of up to 2800 pages per sheet. Microbook is a registered trademark for ultrafiche. Microreproductions on film may be in either positive or negative image. A positive has opaque characters on a clear background. A negative has clear characters on an opaque background.

An *original work in microform* is one in which the matter that is reproduced is prepared specifically for microform production and has not appeared previously as an original work.

Specific Designators

When the specific designator is not used in context with the medium designator "Microform" (e.g., when a microform accompanies a work in a different medium) an ambiguity in medium may occur. In such cases, the combining form "micro" is added to the specific designator to identify its medium: microcard, microcartridge, microcassette, microfiche, microreel, ultramicrofiche.

Microform Cataloging

There are two methods of cataloging a microform.

A microform may be treated as an issue (*AACR* 152C) or version (*AACR* 156A,B) of the work it reproduces, or as a book if it is an original work in microform (*AACR* 156C). It is recorded as a note, (i.e., a part of the description in the cataloging of the work as a book) and does not appear in the catalog as a separate microform entity under its own main entry. If this method is used, the information given in the note should include the Medium designator, Imprint, Collation, and necessary supplementary description in accordance with the rules explained in this section (see Card 83).

A microform may be treated as a work in an audiovisual medium and be cataloged as a separate entity in accordance with the Basic Rules as discussed in this section. This method of cataloging microforms is preferred.

MAIN ENTRY (Area 1)

A microform that is a reproduction of a work, either in book or audiovisual format, is entered in the same manner as the original.

For original works in microform apply Basic Rules IV.A-C, p. 4.

A. Title Main Entry. Title main entry is usually preferred for original works in microform.

B. Series Title Main Entry. When microforms are issued in series or sets, each is usually cataloged under its own title, and an added entry is made for the series title. Main entry under series title may be made in certain instances as explained in Basic Rules IV.B1-3, p. 5.

C. Creator Main Entry. Main entry may be made under the name of the person or corporate body primarily responsible for preparing the copy for an original work in microform *if the name is significant in identifying the work.* The compiler of a collection of copy created by several persons for microform reproduction is not regarded as a creator. The work is entered under the title, the compiler may be cited in the Statement of creator responsibility or in a note, and an added entry may be made for his name.

TITLE/MEDIUM DESIGNATOR/STATEMENT OF CREATOR RESPONSIBILITY (Area 2)

A. Title. Apply Basic Rules V.A1-10, p. 7. The title is taken from the microform itself. In reel, cartridge, and cassette film, the title usually appears in a title frame. When more than one title is given, the title is taken from the frame closest to the subject content. In microforms in sheet (fiche, ultrafiche) or card format, the title usually appears in the top margin. In aperture cards, the title is usually recorded on the data card and may also appear on the microfilm insert. If no title appears in these positions, the title may be taken from a label on the microform mount or on the container. If no title is found, one may be supplied by the cataloger and shown in brackets.

B. Medium Designator. Apply Basic Rule V.B1, p. 10. The general physical form designator (medium designator) "Microform" is given in the singular form following the Title statement and is usually enclosed in brackets. The brackets may be omitted.

C. Statement of Creator Responsibility. Apply Basic Rule V.C, p. 13. Names of authors of textual copy, compilers, artists, photographers, etc., may be cited *if they are significant in identifying an original work in microform.*

EDITION (Area 3)

Apply Basic Rule VI, p. 14, (see Card 81).

IMPRINT (Area 4)*

Place: Producer, copyright/production date; sponsored by Sponsor; Place: Distributed/Released by Distributor, release date.

Apply Basic Rules VII.A-C, p. 15.

COLLATION (PHYSICAL DESCRIPTION) (Area 5)

Number of aperture card(s)/card(s)/cartridge(s)/cassette(s)/fiche/reel(s)/ultrafiche: black and white/color; height × width in centimeters of aperture mount(s) card(s) sheet(s)/width in millimeters of film in cartridge(s) cassette(s) reel(s); other physical characteristics.

*The first statement under Imprint, Collation, and Series, shows all the elements in each area as they would be recorded on the catalog card.

A. Number of Items and Specific Designator

25 aperture cards:	4 cards:	1 cartridge:
2 cassettes:	3 fiche:	1 reel:
2 ultrafiche:		

Give the number of items and the specific designator that identifies the format of the microform. Since the diameter of microfilm reels is usually 3 inches (8 cm.) it need not be given. If the reel is other than 3 inches, note the diameter after the specific designator.

1 reel, 5 in. (13 cm.):

E. Color Statement. The abbreviation "b&w" is used for microforms in black and white, "col." for those in color. Since the majority of microforms are black and white, the color statement may be omitted (see Card 81) except when the microform is in color.

F. Size. Give the height times the width of aperture mounts and cards in centimeters using the abbreviation "cm.", of fiche and ultrafiche sheets in millimeters using the abbreviation "mm.", the width of cartridge, cassette, and reel film in millimeters, using the abbreviation "mm" (16mm, 35mm).

J. Other Physical Characteristics. Give a brief description of other physical characteristics that may be pertinent to the storage or utilization of the microforms, such as the type and dimensions of the container, negative reproduction, etc. Positive reproductions need not be noted.

in box 8 × 13 × 10 cm.
in 5 containers.
negative.

SERIES (Area 6)

(Series title; number within the series: Subseries title; number within the subseries)

Apply Basic Rules IX.A,B, p. 20, (see Card 82).

NOTES (Area 7)

Apply Basic Rules X.A-I, p. 21. Notes are designed to provide supplementary information about the microform(s) not brought out in the formal description. They should be as brief as clarity and good grammar permit, and may be combined and grouped together to create a logical entry. The fullness of detail will vary according to the needs of the particular clientele.

B. Extension of Physical Description. Give any additional information required to convey a more complete picture of the physical properties of the work, or of the special equipment needed to read the microform (see Card 84).

For Readex Microprint reader.
Requires Information Design reader.
Microbook system.

Give the reduction ratio when it is outside the usual range of the specific microform and a special reading device is not designated. The following terms and/or figures may be used to note reduction:

Low reduction, to 16×.
High reduction, 31×-60×.
Very high reduction, 61×-90×.
Ultra high reduction, 100×, 150×, etc. (i.e., the specific reduction above 90×)

If the required reading equipment is designated it is usually not necessary to record the reduction ratio.

D. Other versions. Give the form, Imprint, and Collation of the original work that the microform reproduces. Size may be omitted from the Collation, and total rather than specific pagination may be recorded. The statement may also include title, if different from that of the microform, joint authors, bibliographies, location of the original, and other identifying and/or descriptive information considered necessary (see Cards 81, 82, 84, 85).

Reproduction of book. New York: Bowker, c1970. 397 p.
Reproduction of typescript. Thesis (Ed.D.) College Station, TX: Texas A and M University, 1968. 188 p. Includes bibliography.

I. Contents. Other works reproduced on the microform are identified in the Contents note by author, title, and other essential bibliographic data. Added entries for these works may be made, as appropriate.

OTHER IDENTIFYING AND ORGANIZATIONAL DATA (Area 8)

Apply Basic Rules XI.A-E, p. 24.

D. Media Code. All microforms may be coded under the general designator coding for microforms "NA", or each format may be coded separately under the coding for its specific designator.

Aperture card	NC	Fiche	NH
Card	ND	Reel	NR
Cartridge	NE	Ultrafiche	NU
Cassette	NF		

```
NA
629.45  Apollo 11's moon landing.  [Microform]  Palo
APO        Alto, CA: California Microfilm Co., [1969]
           1 reel: b&w; 35mm.
           SUMMARY: Newspaper and magazine coverage of
        the flight of Apollo 11, July 1969.


        APOLLO PROJECT
```

CARD 80
Microform, reel.
Original work in microform.
Title main entry.
General medium code in call number.
Summary.

```
NH
371.33  National Information Center for Educational Media
NAT        Index to educational slides.  [Microform]
        2d ed.  Los Angeles: University of Southern
        California, c1974.
           7 fiche: 105 x 148 mm; in envelope.
           Reproduction of book.  653 p.
           Also known as the NICEM Index to educational
        slides.

        SLIDES (PHOTOGRAPHY)- CATALOGS/ t: NICEM Index
        to educational slides./ t
```

CARD 81
Microform, fiche.
Creator main entry.
Specific medium code in call number.
Edition statement.
Color statement omitted.
Notes:
Other versions.
Title variations.

```
822     Shirley, James, 1596-1666.
SHI        The gentleman of Venice: a tragi-comedie pre-
        sented at the private house in Salisbury Court
        by Her Majesties servants. [Microform] Written
        by James Shirley. New York: Readex Microprint
        Corp., 1953.
           1 card: 23 x 15 cm. (Three centuries of
        drama: English, 1642-1700)
           Reproduction of book. London: H. Moseley,
        1655. 78 p.

        ENGLISH DRAMA- 17TH CENTURY/ t/ ser

                                          NA:ND
```

CARD 82
Microform, card.
Creator main entry.
Series statement.
Medium code at bottom of card.
Other versions note.

```
822     Shirley, James, 1596-1666.
SHI        The gentleman of Venice : a tragi-comedie
        presented at the private house in Salisbury
        Court by Her Majesties servants / written by
        James Shirley. - London : H. Moseley, 1655.
           78 p. ; 18 cm.
           Microform. New York : Readex Microprint
        Corp., 1953. - 1 card : 23 x 15 cm. - (Three
        centuries of drama : English, 1642-1700)

        ENGLISH DRAMA- 17TH CENTURY/ t/ ser: Three ...
        1700. [Micro             form]
```

CARD 83
Microform cataloged as a version of the original work.
ISBD punctuation.
Added entry for microform series.

```
025.05  Library resources & technical services.  [Micro-
LIB        form]  v.16-   ; Winter-Fall, 1972-
           Ann Arbor, MI: University Microfilms, 1973-

              cartridges: 35mm.
           For Information Design reader.
           Reproduction of the official publication of
        the Resources and Technical Services Division of
        the American Library Association.  Chicago:
        A.L.A.  Quarterly.
        PROCESSING (LIBRARIES)- PERIODICALS/ American
        Library Associa         tion.  Resources and
        Technical Servi         ces Division.
```

CARD 84
Microform, cartridge.
Serial. Open entry.
Notes:
Extension of physical description.
Other versions.

```
942     Challen, W. H.
CHA        Index to Sussex parish registers and bishop
        transcripts.  [Microform]  London: The author,
        1969.
           3 ultrafiche: 105 x 148 mm.
           Reproduction of typescript entitled An index
        to Parish register typescripts, an 86-volume
        register of parishes in London, Midlands, and
        southern counties.

        CHURCH RECORDS AND REGISTERS- ENGLAND/ t: Parish
        register typescripts./ t: Sussex ... trans-
        cripts./ t
```

CARD 85
Microform, ultrafiche.
Creator main entry.
Other versions note.

Medium Designator: **MODEL**

Specific Designators:
Model
Mock-up

Description

A *model* is a three-dimensional representation of a real thing in the exact size of the original or to scale. Included under this designator are unassembled models in do-it-yourself kits and replicas of works of art. A model may or may not be manipulative. A *mock-up* is a representation of a device or process which may be modified for training or analysis to emphasize a particular part or function. A mock-up is usually operable.

MAIN ENTRY (Area 1)

Apply Basic Rules IV.A-C, p. 4.

A. Title Main Entry. Title main entry is preferred.

B. Series Title Main Entry. When models are issued in sets they are usually entered under the title of the set (see Card 87). When single models or sets of models are issued in a series, main entry under series title may be made in accordance with Basic Rules IV.B1-3.

C. Creator Main Entry. A model of a work of art (e.g., a sculpture) or architecture made as a preliminary to the construction of the work itself, may be entered under the name of the person primarily responsible for the artistic design. An added entry is made for the title of the work or the name of the building. However, a replica of a work of art or architecture, which is rarely an exact reproduction of the original, is entered under title. Credit is given to the creator of the original work either in the Title statement, in the Statement of creator responsibility, or in a note, and an added entry is made for his name.

The Thinker by Rodin. [Model] (Title statement)
The Thinker. [Model] Auguste Rodin. (Statement of creator responsibility)
The Thinker. [Model]
A replica of the sculpture in bronze by Auguste Rodin. (Note)

TITLE/MEDIUM DESIGNATOR/STATEMENT OF CREATOR RESPONSIBILITY (Area 2)

A. Title. Apply Basic Rules V.A1-10, p. 7. The title of a model may appear on a label or tag, on its container, or in accompanying literature. If variations occur, the most appropriate title is selected, and a

Source of title note is given (see Basic Rule X.E1, p. 22). If no title is found in these sources or in the producer's catalog or other reference works, one may be supplied by the cataloger, enclosed in brackets.

B. Medium Designator. Apply Basic Rule V.B1, p. 10. The general physical form designator (medium designator) "Model" is given in the singular form following the Title statement and is usually enclosed in square brackets. The brackets may be omitted.

C. Statement of Creator Responsibility. Apply Basic Rule V.C, p. 13. The person(s) (e.g., consultant(s), or organization(s)), responsible for researching the data needed (e.g., historical or scientific facts) to create the model may be cited in the Statement of creator responsibility.

EDITION (Area 3)

No edition statement should be needed. Models are not issued in different "editions".

IMPRINT (Area 4)*

Place: Producer, copyright/production date; sponsored by Sponsor; Place: Distributed/Released by Distributor, release date.

Apply Basic Rules VII.A-C, p. 15.

COLLATION (PHYSICAL DESCRIPTION) (Area 5)

Number of model(s)/mock-up(s): number of pieces/various pieces; color/specific color; height × width × depth in centimeters; description of container, height × width × depth of container in centimeters/ mount/other physical characteristics.

A. Number of Items and Specific Designator

5 models: 1 mock-up:

In simplified cataloging, if the entry describes only one model, the number and the specific designator "model" may be omitted since it is the same as the general designator.

---

*The first statement under Imprint, Collation, and Series, shows all the elements in each area as they would be recorded on the catalog card.

B. Physical Contents. If practical, a brief listing of the number and names of detachable parts, or separate pieces needed to make the model, may be recorded. When a long list or detailed description is required, the phrase "various pieces" is substituted for the enumeration in the Collation statement and the parts are described in a note (see Card 88).

E. Color Statement. The abbreviation "col." is used if the model is in more than one color. The specific color is given if the model is in one color only.

3 models: 6 pieces; col;
1 mock-up: various pieces; brown;

F. Size. If readily available, give the height × width × depth of the model in centimeters, using the abbreviation "cm."

J. Other Physical Characteristics. A brief description may be given of the type and size of the container, the mounting, or any other physical properties considered important. When the description cannot be succinctly stated, the information should be given in a note instead of in the Collation.

SERIES (Area 6)

(Series title; number within the series: Subseries title; number within the subseries)

Apply Basic Rules IX.A,B, p. 20.

NOTES (Area 7)

Apply Basic Rules X.A-I, p. 21.

B. Extension of Physical Description. Give the scale, if known, and any additional information required to convey a more complete picture of the physical properties involved in the utilization and functioning of the model (see Card 86).

Scale 1:16.
Four times actual size.
Removable parts.
Battery operated.

H. Summary. A summary which combines the supplementary information often given in several separate notes, may provide a sufficiently clear and brief description. The caption "SUMMARY" may be omitted (see Cards 87-89).

OTHER IDENTIFYING AND ORGANIZATIONAL DATA (Area 8)

Apply Basic Rules XI.A-E, p. 24.

D. Media Code. All models may be coded under the general designator coding for models, "EA", or each format may be coded separately under the coding for the specific designator.

Mock-up	EM
Model	EE

```
EA
611     Ear - anatomy of hearing.  [Model]  Oak Lawn, IL:
EAR        Ideal School Supply Co., [196-?]
           1 model: col; 16 x 32 x 3 cm; in plastic case,
        17 x 34 x 6 cm.
           Four times actual size.
           With instructional guide.
           The parts of the ear are painted to show the
        anatomical structure.

        EAR
```

CARD 86
Model.
Title main entry.
General medium code in call number.
Notes:
Extension of physical description.
Accompanying and/or descriptive material.
Summary (caption omitted).

EE
612.6 HUM

Human development models. [Model] Chicago: Nystrom, [196-]
5 models: col; in plastic carrying case.
With teacher's guide.
SUMMARY: The models illustrate the significant stages of human development from fertilization through five months. Two models are removable for closer examination.
CONTENTS: Sperm cells in uterus.- 2 week embryo.- 7- to 8-week fetus.- 13-week fetus.- 18- to 20-week fetus.
GROWTH/ REPRODUCTION

CARD 87
Set of models.
Set title main entry.
Specific medium code in call number.

Notes:
Accompanying and/or descriptive material.
Summary.
Contents.

523.4 SOL

Solar system simulator. [Model] Northbrook, IL: Hubbard, [196-?]
1 model: various pieces; col; 12 x 22 x 8 in. (31 x 51 x 21 cm.) mounted on round calibrated base.
With study guide, including planet position tables.
The planets, suspended on rods around the 6-inch diameter sun, are identified by color, size, and distance, and can be set by month to show their relative positions.
PLANETS

CARD 88
Model.
Title main entry.
Size in inches and centimeters.

Notes:
Accompanying and/or descriptive material.
Summary (caption omitted).

```
651.8   Eduputer.  [Model]  Programming Sciences Corp.,
EDU        1970.
           1 mock-up: 73 x 73 x 65 cm; in metal casing.
           With instructor and student guides, 16 taped
        lectures, cassette recorder, course guide: 4v.
           A console control panel that simulates the
        operation of the IBM model 2030 console to give
        hands-on experience in performing computer
        operator functions.

        COMPUTERS/ IBM 2030 (COMPUTER)
```

```
                                            EA:EM
```

CARD 89
Mock-up.
Title main entry.
Medium code at bottom of card.
Place omitted.
Notes:
- **Accompanying and/or descriptive material.**
- **Summary (caption omitted).**

Medium Designator: MOTION PICTURE

Specific Designators:
- Cartridge
- Cassette
- Loop
- Reel

Description

A *motion picture* is a series of still pictures on film, with or without sound, designed to be projected in rapid succession to produce the optical effect of motion. The terms "motion picture" and "film" are often used interchangeably.

Motion pictures are produced in a variety of sizes (8, 16, 35, 55, and 70mm) and formats (cartridge, cassette, loop, and reel). A *cartridge* film is a loop film enclosed in a cartridge; a *cassette* film is mounted in reel-to-reel format and enclosed in a cassette; a *loop* is a short section of film, not enclosed, which has the ends spliced together and is designed to run continuously; *reel* films run from reel to reel. A *kinescope* is a motion picture taken from a television screen and is usually mounted on a reel. It is cataloged in the same manner as a reel film, and the fact that it is a kinescope recording is given in a note (see Summary p. 23).

Specific Designators

When the specific designator is used out of context with the medium designator "Motion picture" (e.g., in an identifying or descriptive statement in which there is no reference to its medium designator) an ambiguity in medium may occur. In such cases, the medium designator itself is used in conjunction with the specific designator to identify its medium: motion picture cartridge, motion picture cassette, motion picture loop, motion picture reel.

MAIN ENTRY (Area 1)

A. Title Main Entry. Apply Basic Rule IV.A, p. 4. As a general rule, motion pictures are entered under title since the extent of collaborative contribution makes it difficult to attribute to one person or corporate body the overall responsibility for the creation of the work.

B. Series Title Main Entry. Apply Basic Rule IV.B, p. 5. When motion pictures are issued in series or sets, each film is usually cataloged under its own title, and an added entry is made for the series title. The series title may be used for the main entry when the individual film title is dependent upon the series title for meaning, or when the individual film is a part of a longer film which has been cut into single-concept units. When the series title becomes the main entry title, the title of each individual unit is treated as a subtitle of the series title and an added entry is made for the title of the individual film if it is sufficiently meaningful to stand alone (see Card 104).

Individual title:	Nervous system
Series title:	Human body
Series title main entry:	Human body: Nervous system

When several motion pictures are entered *collectively* under the series title, the titles of the individual films are given in a Contents note. An added entry is made for each individual film title if it is distinctive (see Card 106). When each film presents an aspect of the same subject and there are so many titles in the set that their listing would require several continuation cards, a briefer entry may be made by giving a summary of the content of all the films instead of a Contents note (see Card 105).

C. Creator Main Entry. Apply Basic Rule IV.C, p. 6. A motion picture is rarely entered under the name of a creator because of the difficulty in establishing a creativity priority among the many functions performed in the production of a film. If, however, the major portion of the intellectual and artistic content is clearly the work of a person *whose name is significant in identifying the film,* creator main entry may be used. An added entry is made for the title (see Card 95). Creator main entry will occur more frequently in 8mm films which are less complicated to produce than are 16mm motion pictures and which require the services of fewer people. Many 8mm films are the work of one or two persons, and many are locally produced as an incentive to learning. If there is any doubt as to creatorship, enter the motion picture under title and make added entries for creators, as appropriate.

The motion picture version of a written work is not usually entered under the author of the original work since it is extremely doubtful that the film is an exact reproduction. Title main entry is used, and an author or author-title added entry is made for the work on which the motion picture is based. Some media centers may elect to enter the motion picture version of a written work under its author if learning objectives are better accomplished by keeping together all formats and interpretations of an author's works.

TITLE/MEDIUM DESIGNATOR/STATEMENT OF CREATOR RESPONSIBILITY (Area 2)

A. Title. Apply Basic Rules V.A1-10, p. 7. The title is taken from the motion picture itself. If the film does not provide adequate information, the title is taken from the cartridge or cassette, from accompanying data such as the teacher's guide, producer's catalog, etc., or from the label on the container, and its source may be given in a note (see Source of Title, pp. 22, 156).

If more than one title appears on the film, preference is given the title closest to the subject content. Significant title variations are cited in a note, and added entries may be made for variant titles by which the film may be known (see Title Variations, pp. 8, 22, 156).

B. Medium Designator. Apply Basic Rule V.B1, p. 10. The general physical form designator (medium designator) "Motion picture" is given in the singular form following the Title statement and is usually enclosed in square brackets. The brackets may be omitted (see Basic Rule V.B1, p. 10, and Card 92). In catalogs limited to motion pictures the medium designator in each entry is omitted.

C. Statement of Creator Responsibility. Apply Basic Rule V.C, p. 13. The function(s) performed and the name(s) of the creator(s) are stated after the medium designator *if they are significant in identifying the work*, such as names of well-known producers and directors. If more than three names are listed for any one function, the name cited first is given, followed by the phrase "and others". Added entries may be made for names recorded in the Statement of creator responsibility (see Cards 95, 96). If there is doubt that the names are essential for the identification of the work, the statement of creator responsibility is omitted, and the names may be given in a Credits note.

If creator main entry is used, the function(s) performed and the name of the creator are stated. The names of joint creators are included in the statement if there is a shared responsibility in the performance of the same function(s) (see Cards 95, 96).

EDITION (Area 3)

Apply Basic Rule VI, p. 14. When a motion picture has been revised without a change in title, a simple statement (e.g., 2d ed., Rev. ed.) according to the wording on the film itself, follows the Medium designator/Statement of creator responsibility (see Card 99). If the title has been changed, or additional descriptive detail about the new edition is considered necessary, the Edition statement is omitted and the required information is given in a note (see Card 100).

IMPRINT (Area 4)*

Place: Producer, copyright/production date; sponsored by Sponsor; Place: Distributed/Released by Distributor, release date.

A. Place. Apply Basic Rule VII.A, p. 15. The city of the principal offices of the producer and distributor is noted. Place is not given for a sponsor. If the city is well known the state or country in which it is located need not be noted.

Chicago: Erikson Productions.

*The first statement under Imprint, Collation, and Series, shows all the elements in each area as they would be recorded on the catalog card.

The city and state (in the U.S.) or country (outside the U.S.) are given if there may be doubt as to the location of the city. Abbreviations of State names recommended by the U.S. Postal Service are used (see Appendix IV).*

Paris, MO: Ransdell Films,
Brighton, Eng.: Univ. of Sussex.

If the location is unknown, the probable place followed by a question mark [Chicago?] or the abbreviation "[s.l.]" may be noted (see Card 97); or place may be omitted from the Imprint statement (see Cards 91, 92, 94, 100-107) except where the producer or distributor is located in a country other than that of the cataloging agency.

B. Producer/Sponsor/Distributor. Apply Basic Rules VII.B1-4, p. 16. The name(s) of the producer/sponsor/distributor, as applicable, is given in the briefest form in which it can be understood and identified without ambiguity (see Cards 91, 92). Phrases denoting the function of sponsor and distributor are used as explained in Basic Rules VII.B1-3 (see Cards 90, 93, 95-98). The phrase "Distributed by" or "Released by" which indicates the function of the distributor may be omitted, if desired (see Cards 101-105, 107). The abbreviation "[s.n.]" is used if a producer, sponsor, or distributor cannot be ascertained.

C. Date. Apply Basic Rules VII.C1-4, p. 17. A date is always given, the latest copyright date taking preference over all other dates. The letter "c" preceding the date designates a copyright date. When the only date on the motion picture appears without the copyright symbol "©", it is interpreted as the production date and is noted in the catalog entry without the preceding "c" (see Cards 97, 98). If the date of release is significantly different from the date of copyright, it is recorded after the copyright date and is preceded by the word "released."

Film Associates, c1969; released 1972.

---

*The ALA Catalog Code Revision Committee has reversed its decision to use the U.S. Postal Service State abbreviations and is now recommending that the list as given in the current AACR (Mass., Conn., etc.) be used in the second edition.

If there is both a producer and a distributor, and the date of release by the distributor is significantly different from the date of copyright, the copyright date is given after the producer, and the release date after the distributor (see Cards 101, 102). If no date can be established, a probable date of production should be shown in brackets (see Basic Rule VII.C4, p. 18). The abbreviation "n.d." signifying no indication of date should not be used.

COLLATION (PHYSICAL DESCRIPTION) (Area 5)

Number of cartridge(s)/cassette(s)/loop(s)/reel(s): number of minutes: silent/sound; color/black and white; 8mm/super 8mm/16mm/35mm/55mm/70mm.

A. Number of Items and Specific Designator

3 cartridges: 1 cassette: 4 loops: 1 reel:

C. Length. Give time duration in minutes using the abbreviation "min." If long films are mounted on two or more reels, give the total running time. When the entry includes two or more films, each with the same time duration, give the running time of each (see Cards 94, 96, 105, 106). When the entry includes two or more films with individual titles, give the running time of each if there are only two, e.g., 26, 31 min.: or the span of time if there are more than two, e.g., 26-36 min.; or omit the time in the Collation and include it after each title in the Contents note.

D. Sound Statement. The abbreviation "si." is used for silent films, "sd." for sound films. Since most 16mm motion pictures currently available are sound, the sound statement may be omitted (see Card 92) except for silent 16mm films (see Cards 97, 104-107). If the sound is recorded on a magnetic sound track this fact is given in the Extension of physical description note (see Card 103).

E. Color Statement. The abbreviation "col." is used for color films, "b&w" for black and white prints, "col. and b&w" for color films with black and white sequences, or black and white films with color sequences.

F. Size. Give the width of the film using the abbreviation "mm" for millimeters. For 8mm films it is essential to distinguish between standard and super 8mm formats since each requires a different type of equipment for projection. The super 8 format has smaller sprocket holes and a sixty percent larger image, and the cartridge of a super 8 film differs from that of a standard 8. Super 8mm is always designated (see Cards 101-103, 105-107). The notation "8mm" indicates standard 8mm format (see Cards 101, 104).

In motion picture catalogs, the sound, color, and size elements of the physical description that are common to the majority of the films may be omitted in each entry if an explanatory statement is provided at the beginning of the catalog.

Unless otherwise indicated, all titles are 16mm sound color motion pictures.

SERIES (Area 6)

(Series title; number within the series: Subseries title; number within the subseries)

Apply Basic Rules IX.A,B, p. 20. Give the series title in parentheses following the Collation, in the form in which it appears on the work itself (see Cards 90-94, 105, 107). Include the number of the film in the series, if given, and considered necessary for sequential purposes (see Card 107).

1 reel: 10 min; sd; col; 16mm. (Government story; no. 15)

When main entry is under series title, the Series statement is omitted unless the motion picture(s) is part of another series, or is a subseries (see Card 105).

NOTES (Area 7)

Apply Basic Rules X.A-I, p. 21. Notes are designed to provide supplementary information about the film not brought out in the formal description. They should be as brief as clarity and good grammar permit, and may be combined or grouped together to create a clear informational and descriptive statement. The fullness of detail will vary according to the needs of the particular clientele.

A. Educational Level. The educational level for which the film is intended is indicated following the Series area (see Cards 95, 96, 100). It may, however, be omitted if desired, or if a wide discrepancy occurs in the level assigned in descriptive sources. Educational level terms, abbreviations, and conditions under which the information is given in a note, will be found in Basic Rule X.A, p. 21.

B. Extension of Physical Description. When the physical format requires the use of special equipment, give the information that indicates the kind of equipment needed (see Card 103).

Requires Cinemascope lens.
Magnetic sound track.
Kodak projection cartridge.

C. Accompanying and/or Descriptive Material. Material accompanying the film which is designed to assist in its presentation or understanding is described (see Cards 90-93, 99-105, 107).

With teacher's guide.
With instructor's guide, and student syllabus with audiocassette.

D. Other Versions. Each version of a motion picture in the collection is cataloged separately. To minimize repetitive cataloging, the various versions in the collection may be listed on one card. Give sufficient information to identify differences in physical characteristics and location (see Card 102).

Other versions in the same or a different medium that are not in the collection and are known to exist may be noted (see Cards 94-97, 103, 104); or all known versions may be listed on one card (see Card 101).

Spanish version also issued.
Videotape also issued.
Issued in 8mm and super 8mm cartridge.

E1. Source of Title. Note the source of the title if it is not taken from the motion picture itself.

Title from label on container.

E2. Title Variations. Record the original title if it is known to be different, and any other title under which the film was released.

French version released in Canada under the title Le festin des morts.
Previously released under the title Julie, the wise librarian.

If the film is popularly known under a shortened or variant title, this title is noted and an added entry is made for it.

F. Related Works. Other works upon which the film depends for its intellectual or artistic content are cited in a note, and appropriate added entries are made (see Cards 90, 91, 93, 101, 102).

Based on a story by Leo Tolstoi.
Based on the book of the same title by Gilbert Fites.

G. Credits. Give the names of individuals or organizations who have contributed significantly to the creation of the film and have not been noted in the statement of creator responsibility. The Credits note may include any of the following participants whose work might be considered of special importance in the production of a film:

producer (if not named in the Imprint. Associate, assistant, executive producer if no producer is given);
director (assistant director if no director is given);
writer of the story, screenplay, script, adaptation, or narration;
artist whose work is reproduced;
narrator or commentator; voices;
consultant;
creator of animation;
composer, music director, arranger of orchestration;
photographer or cameraman;
film editor.

How many and which of these names are cited will depend upon the requirements of the patrons served. If given, the names are cited in the order in which they appear on the film. The function or contribution is noted, followed by the person's name (see Cards 90, 93). Added entries may be made as considered necessary.

CREDITS: Director, Sidney Goldsmith; speaker, Walter Massey.

The caption "CREDITS" may be omitted (see Cards 94-97, 99, 101, 102, 104, 105).

The listing of names in the cast of a motion picture may be given in the Credits note (see Card 97) or in a separate note with the caption "CAST". As a general rule, only the names of featured actors are given.

CREDITS: Producers, Paul Emerson, John Fernald; directors, Paul Lee, Val Drumm; music, Richard Newson; cast, Clive Francis, Angela Scoular.

H. Summary. The Summary should provide a brief, accurate and objective statement concerning the subject of the film, sufficient to guide the potential user in the initial selection of appropriate material.

The content should be summarized in fifty words or less. Avoid repeating the title and subtitle, or any information adequately expressed by them. Omit statements which do not contribute to an understanding of the content, and avoid promotional or evaluative terms. Short phrases should be used when they will substitute adequately for complete sentences, but clarity must not be sacrificed for brevity.

References to techniques used in the production of the film (e.g., kinescope recording, time lapse photography, slow motion, animation, iconography, microphotography, etc.) may be given when this information is significant (see Cards 95, 96, 99-102). The caption "SUMMARY" may be omitted (see Cards 90-103, 105, 107).

I. Contents. If a film consists of a number of parts, or the entry includes a number of films, each of which has a distinctive title, these titles are given in a Contents note. The running time is noted after each title if it has not been recorded in the Collation. Title added entries may be made as considered necessary (see Card 106).

OTHER IDENTIFYING AND ORGANIZATIONAL DATA (Area 8)

Apply Basic Rules XI.A-E, p. 24.

A. Standard Numbering (SN). A ten digit identification number, similar in format to the International Standard Book Number (ISBN), is now being assigned to each version of every 16mm educational film.

The *Standard Number* consists of four units of information: 1) group identifier; 2) producer prefix; 3) unique title number; 4) check digit.

The *group identifier* "0" indicates that the principal office of the film's producer is in the United Kingdom, the United States of America, Eire, Australia or South Africa.

The *producer prefix* has from two to six digits, with the larger producers having the smaller numbers.

A unique *title number* is assigned to every variation of each title (long version, short version, black & white print; color print, revision, etc.).

The tenth digit is known as the *check digit*, and is mathematically calculated by a formula known as Modulus 11. The check digit almost precludes the possibility that any digit in the Standard Number could be inverted or transcribed incorrectly without being detected when the information is keyboarded into the computer.

Group Identifier	Producer Prefix	Title Number	Check Digit
0	-01	-047523	-0

A Standard Number is recorded on Card 90A, supplied as an example of how an assigned Standard Number would appear in the catalog entry. When Standard Numbering is established for all types of nonprint materials, consideration may be given to including the Standard Number in the Notes area, conforming to the position prescribed for the International Standard Book Number in the *International Standard Bibliographic Description (Monographs)*.

B. Tracings. To facilitate access to motion pictures through the catalog or computer, appropriate subject headings and added entries should be assigned. The tracings, which are usually placed at the bottom of the card, constitute a record of the subject and added entries made for the film. Tracings also alert the user to subject headings under which he may find additional material.

1. *Subject headings.* Subject headings for motion pictures should be selected from the same approved subject heading list that is used for the book collection (see Basic Rule XI.B1, p. 24). All new and alternative terms that are considered necessary for local needs and specialized collections must be noted for future use.

2. *Added entries.* Added entries should be made for those personal and corporate names, original and variant titles, and series titles under which a user might search for the film. Added entries for sponsors are not usually made, and those for producers are optional.

C. Classification Number. Motion picture collections may be organized by subject content and classified by the Library of Congress or Dewey Decimal systems. It is generally considered desirable to shelve large collections of reel film by a simple sequential accession number system. The shelving and retrieval of 16mm sound reel films may be facilitated by storing together reels of the same size which hold film of approximately the same length. A 400-foot reel is considered "one reel"; other sizes are increments of this. Thus an 800-foot reel is "two reels", a 1200-foot reel is "three reels", etc. By using the prefix numbers, 1, 2, 3, etc., to indicate the number of reels that would be needed for the film footage, reels may easily be separated by size. In this system the films are shelved first by prefix number and then by accession number (see Card 92).

400' (one reel) films are numbered beginning with 1-001
800' (two reel) films are numbered beginning with 2-001
1200' (three reel) films are numbered beginning with 3-001

In the same manner, the medium coding for each format may also be used as a prefix if like formats are to be kept together (see Media Code).

MP 1-001, MP-2-001, MP 3-001 for reel films
ML 001 for loop films
MR 001 for cartridge films
MC 001 for cassette films

D. Media Code. Automated procedures generally require that medium designators be coded. The same code should be used in manual systems if codification is desired. For informational purposes, the coding for the general and specific designators may be shown at the bottom of the card (see Cards 92, 105).

1. *General and specific designator code.* The several formats of motion pictures may be coded under the general designator coding for motion pictures "MA" or each format may be coded separately under the coding for its specific designator.

Cartridge	MR
Cassette	MC
Loop	ML
Reel	MP

2. *Media code and designators in the call number.* When motion pictures are stored in a separate area, the medium coding or designator may be placed above the classification number to serve as a location device (see Card 91). The format distinctions needed for shelving and retrieval will determine whether general or specific designators spelled out in full or the medium coding should be used.

3. *Color code.* The color coding of catalog cards to indicate that the work is a motion picture or is in a nonbook format is not recommended.

E. Additional Information. Some catalogs may require the inclusion of additional information such as purchase price, rental rate, regional or cooperative location, shelf number, Standard Account Number (SAN), etc. The position of this information in the catalog entry is not prescribed, but should be given in an appropriate area. For example, purchase price and rental rate may be noted after the date in the Imprint area or following the Standard Number.

```
MA
973.3   Valley Forge.  [Motion picture]  New York: Steve
VAL        Krantz Productions; Chicago: Released by En-
           cyclopaedia Britannica Educational Corp., c1972.
           1 reel: 7 min; sd; col; 16mm.  (War for
        Independence)
           With teacher's guide.
           Adapted from the 1962 filmstrip of the same
        title.
           CREDITS: Adaptation, William Peltz; collabo-
        rator, John C. Miller.
           SUMMARY: Contrasts the hardships experienced

                                     (See next card)
```

CARD 90
Motion picture: 16mm, reel.
Title main entry.
Fully detailed cataloging.
General medium code in call number.
Producer/Distributor.
Various notes.

(Card 2)

MA
973.3 Valley Forge. [Motion picture]
VAL

by Washington's troops in Valley Forge during the winter of 1777-78 and the comforts of the British troops in Philadelphia, and emphasizes the resultant damage to American morale.

SN 0-01-047523-0

U.S.- HISTORY- REVOLUTION/ VALLEY FORGE, PA/ ser

CARD 90A
Continuation card.
Standard Number (supplied as an example).

MP
973.3 Valley Forge. [Motion picture] Steve Krantz
VAL Productions; EBEC, c1972.

1 reel: 7 min; sd; col; 16mm. (War for Independence)

With teacher's guide.

Adapted from the 1962 filmstrip.

Contrasts the hardships experienced by Washington's troops in Valley Forge during the winter of 1777-78 and the comforts of the British troops in Philadelphia, and emphasizes the resultant damage to American morale.

U.S.- HISTORY- REVOLUTION/ VALLEY FORGE, PA/ ser

CARD 91
Motion picture: 16mm, reel.
Title main entry.
Moderately detailed cataloging.
Specific medium code in call number.
Place omitted.

```
1-101   Valley Forge. Motion picture. EBEC, c1972.
           1 reel: 7 min; col; 16mm. (War for Indepen-
        dence)
           Teacher's guide.
           Describes the hardships experienced by Wash-
        ington's troops in Valley Forge and the damage
        to American morale.


        U.S.- HISTORY- REVOLUTION/ VALLEY FORGE, PA/ ser

                                            MA:MP
```

CARD 92
Motion picture: 16mm, reel.
Title main entry.
Simplified cataloging.
Accession number classification.
Medium code at bottom of card.
Medium designator without brackets.

```
973.3   Valley Forge / [Motion picture]. - New York :
VAL        Steve Krantz Productions ; Chicago : Released
           by Encyclopaedia Britannica Educational Corp.,
           c1972.
           1 reel : 7 min. ; sd. ; col. ; 16mm. - (War
        for Independence)
           With teacher's guide.
           Adapted from the 1962 filmstrip of the same
        title.
           CREDITS: Adaptation, William Peltz; collabo-
        rator, John C. Miller.

                                     (See next card)
```

CARD 93
Motion picture: 16mm, reel.
Title main entry.
ISBD punctuation
(Card 1 shown only).

389 The Metric system. Part 1, 2. [Motion picture]
MET Victor Kayfetz Productions, c1972.
2 reels: 13 min. each; sd; col; 16mm. (Metric system)
Also issued in super 8mm cartridge.
Educational consultant, Herbert Siegel.
Discusses and compares the English and metric systems and shows decimal calculating.

DECIMAL SYSTEM/ METRIC SYSTEM/ WEIGHTS AND MEASURES- GREAT BRITAIN/ ser

CARD 94
Motion picture: 16mm, reel.
Title main entry.
A work in 2 parts.
Other versions note.
Credits, Summary (captions omitted).

551 Hubley, John
HUB Dig: a journey into the earth. [Motion picture] Written, designed, and produced by John and Faith Hubley. New York: Released by Film Images/Radim Films, c1972.
1 reel: 25 min; sd; col; 16mm. K-J.
Also issued as 3 separate consecutive films, and in 35mm.
Music, Quincy Jones.
An animated film in which a boy and his dog travel through geologic time.
GEOLOGY/ PHYSICAL GEOGRAPHY/ Hubley, Faith/ t

CARD 95
Motion picture: 16mm, reel.
Creator main entry.
Statement of creator responsibility.
Educational level note.

551 DIG

Dig: a journey into the earth. [Motion picture]
Written, designed, and produced by John and Faith Hubley. New York: Released by Film Images/Radim Films, c1972.
3 reels: 27 min; sd; col; 16mm. K-J.
Also issued as one continuous film, and in 35mm.
Music, Quincy Jones.
Animated films in which a boy and his dog travel through geologic time.
GEOLOGY/ PHYSICAL GEOGRAPHY/ Hubley, Faith/ Hubley, John

CARD 96
Motion picture: 16mm, reel.
Title main entry.
Several films made from one film.
Statement of creator responsibility.

791.43 ADV

The Adventures of Dollie. [Motion picture]
[s.l.]: American Mutoscope and Biograph Co., 1908; Davenport, IA: Released by Blackhawk Films/Eastin-Phelan Corp., [1970?]
1 reel: 15 min; si; b&w; 16mm.
Also issued in standard and super 8mm.
Originally released in 35mm.
Director, D.W. Griffith; cast, Linda Arvidson, Arthur Johnson, Charles Inslee.
A melodrama about a gypsy who kidnaps a young girl.

MOVING PICTURES 

CARD 97
Motion picture: 16mm, reel.
Title main entry.
Place unknown.
Production date.
Probable release date.

B STE

Adlai Stevenson. [Motion picture] London: BBC-TV; New York: Distributed by Time-Life Films, 1967.

1 reel: 30 min; sd; b&w; 16mm.

Mr. Stevenson discusses his aspirations, his family, and events in his life in an interview on the BBC television series Face to face.

STEVENSON, ADLAI EWING/ British Broadcasting Corporation. Television Service.

CARD 98
Motion picture: 16mm, reel.
Title main entry.
Foreign producer.
Production date.
Producer added entry.

612 CIR

Circulation and the human body. [Motion picture] Rev. ed. Los Angeles: Churchill Films, c1972.

1 reel: 11 min; sd; col; 16mm.

With study guide.

Director, Donald MacDonald; animator, Spencer Peel.

Uses animation to explain how the heart and circulatory system service the needs of the body's cells.

BLOOD- CIRCULATION/ HEART

CARD 99
Motion picture: 16mm, reel.
Title main entry.
Edition statement.

```
551.4   Exploring the ocean.  [Motion picture]  Churchill
EXP        Films, c1972.
           1 reel: 14 min; sd; col; 16mm.  I-J.
           With study guide.
           Revised version of the 1960 motion picture of
        the same title with projector stops for discus-
        sion inserted.
           Uses animation to describe the topography,
        geology, flora and fauna of the ocean.  Includes
        a discussion of pollution.

        OCEAN/ POLLUTION
```

CARD 100
Motion picture: 16mm, reel.
Title main entry.
Educational level note.
Edition note.

```
973     An American time capsule.  [Motion picture]
AME        Charles Braverman, c1968; Pyramid Films, 1969.
           3 min; sd; col.
           Versions available: cartridge, 8mm, super 8mm;
        reel, 8mm, 16mm, 35mm.
           With teacher's guide.
           Originally shown on the Smothers Brothers
        television program.
           Music, Sandy Nelson; editor, Ken Rudolph.
           A kinestasis film.  Uses kaleidoscopic views
        of still pictures to summarize two hundred years
        of American history.
        U.S.- HISTORY
```

CARD 101
Motion picture.
Title main entry.
Composite card for all available versions.

973
AME

An American time capsule. [Motion picture]
Charles Braverman, c1968; Pyramid Films, 1969.
1 reel: 3 min; sd; col; 35mm.
With teacher's guide.
Also in collection: cartridge, super 8mm; reel, 16mm.
Originally shown on the Smothers Brothers television program.
Music, Sandy Nelson; editor, Ken Rudolph.
A kinestasis film. Uses kaleidoscopic views of still pictures to summarize two hundred years of American his tory.
U.S.- HISTORY

CARD 102
Motion picture: 35mm, reel.
Title main entry.
Composite card for versions in the collection.

623.89
NAV

Navigation - tool of discovery. [Motion picture]
Stanton Films; Doubleday Multimedia, c1969.
1 reel: 18 min; sd; col; super 8mm.
Magnetic sound track.
With teacher's guide.
Also issued in b&w.
Traces the history of navigation from the time of the Phoenician traders through the days of Captain James Cook.

NAVIGATION- HISTORY

CARD 103
Motion picture: super 8mm, reel.
Title main entry.
Extension of physical description note.

MR
796.9 Skiing. No.5: Stem turn. [Motion picture] Cal-
SKI-5 vin Productions; Athletic Institute, c1969.
1 cartridge: 4 min; si; col; 8mm.
With guide.
Also issued in super 8mm cartridge.
Consultant, Cyrus Smythe; demonstrators, Paul Mascotti, and others.

SKIS AND SKIING/ t: Stem turn.

CARD 104
Motion picture: standard 8mm, cartridge.
Series title main entry.
Specific medium code in call number.

796.4 Rings. [Motion picture]. Calvin Productions;
RIN Athletic Institute, c1970.
9 cartridges: 4 min. each; si; col; super 8mm. (Men's gymnastics)
With guide.
Consultant, Newton Loken; demonstrators, Univ. of Michigan Gymnastics Team.
Each film demonstrates a different technique.

RINGS (GYMNASTICS)/ ser

MA:MR

CARD 105
Motion picture set: super 8mm, cartridge.
Subseries title main entry.
Series statement.
Medium code at bottom of card.

912 Map reading. [Motion picture] Hubbard Scienti-
MAP fic Co., c1972.
5 cartridges: 4 min. each; si; col; super 8mm.
Earth and scale.- Longitude and latitude.- Map projection.- Contour mapping.- Profile mapping.

MAPS/ t: contents

CARD 106
Motion picture set: super 8mm, cartridge.
Series title main entry.
Contents note (caption omitted).
Title added entry for each title in Contents note.

943.087 Berlin Wall. [Motion picture] Dennis Grogan;
BER Thorne Films, c1971.
1 cartridge: 4 min; si; b&w; super 8mm. (8mm documents project; no. 388)
Notes on cartridge container.
A documentary showing scenes of sealing the border between East and West Germany, and of an actual escape attempt.

BERLIN WALL/ ser

CARD 107
Motion picture: super 8mm, cartridge.
Title main entry.
Number within series in series statement.

Medium Designator: **PICTURE**

Specific Designators:

Art original	Post card
Art print	Poster
Hologram	Stereograph
Photograph	Study print
Picture	

Description

A *picture* is a representation made on opaque material by drawing, painting, photography, or other techniques of graphic art. An *art original* is the picture originally created by the artist. An *art print* is a printed reproduction of a work of art. A *hologram* is a three-dimensional image produced by laser photography. A *photograph* is an image produced on a sensitized surface by the action of light. The term "*photograph*" indicates either the picture produced directly from developed film, or a printed reproduction of that picture. A *poster* is a large illustration designed for display. A *stereograph* is a pair of pictures presented to give a three-dimensional effect when viewed through a stereoscope. A *study print* is a picture, generally with accompanying text, prepared specifically for teaching purposes.

Pictures are issued singly and in sets. Miscellaneous pictures that are of temporary value are usually treated as vertical file material, and are arranged by subject.

MAIN ENTRY (Area 1)

Apply Basic Rules IV.A-C, p. 4.

A. Title Main Entry. Title main entry is usually preferred, except for art originals and art prints (see Creator Main Entry).

B. Series Title Main Entry. When pictures are issued in sets they are usually entered under the title of the set. Added entries may be made for the artists and/or titles of the individual pictures if they are considered especially significant. When one picture in a set is cataloged as a separate entity, its title is treated as a subtitle of the set title and is brought out in the catalog as an added entry.

When sets of pictures are issued in a series, main entry under series title may be made in accordance with Basic Rules IV.B1-3, p. 5.

C. Creator Main Entry. An art original is entered under the name of the artist. If the identity of the artist is in doubt (e.g., a painting attributed to, or in the style of an artist) the work is entered under title. An art print or set of art prints that reproduces the work(s) of an artist is entered under his name (see Card 108), especially when it is desirable to keep together all formats that illustrate his work. An added entry is made for the title of the art print, and for the title of the original work if it differs from that of the print.

A compiler of a set of pictures is not regarded as a creator. The pictures are entered under the title of the set, the compiler may be cited in the Statement of creator responsibility or in a note, and an added entry may be made for his name.

TITLE/MEDIUM DESIGNATOR/STATEMENT OF CREATOR RESPONSIBILITY (Area 2)

A. Title. Apply Basic Rules V.A1-10, p. 7. The title is taken from the face, margin, mat, or verso of the picture. If the title for a set or series does not appear on the individual pictures, it is usually taken from the container or from accompanying material. If no title is found, one may be supplied by the cataloger and shown in brackets.

B. Medium Designator. Apply Basic Rule V.B1, p. 10. The general physical form designator (medium designator) "Picture" is given in the singular form following the Title statement and is usually enclosed in brackets. The brackets may be omitted. (See Card 113).

C. Statement of Creator Responsibility. Apply Basic Rule V.C, p. 13. Names of illustrators, photographers, compilers, authors of textual matter, etc., may be cited *if they are significant in identifying the work.*

EDITION (Area 3)

Apply Basic Rule VI, p. 14.

IMPRINT (Area 4)*

Place: Producer, copyright/production date; sponsored by Sponsor; Place: Distributed/Released by Distributor, release date.

Apply Basic Rules VII.A-C, p. 15. The items of information in the Imprint for commercially or locally produced works do not apply to an art original. Instead, the artist's country and the year the work was completed, or the span of years during which the work was in process, may be noted.

*The first statement under Imprint, Collation, and Series, shows all the elements in each area as they would be recorded on the catalog card.

Boucher, François
The love letter. [Picture] France, 1750.

COLLATION (PHSYICAL DESCRIPTION) (Area 5)

Number of art original(s)/art print(s)/hologram(s)/photograph(s)/picture(s)/post cards/posters(s)/stereograph(s)/study print(s): color/black and white; height x width in centimeters & audio accompaniment(s); other physical characteristics.

A. Number of Items and Specific Designator

1 art original;	1 art print;	3 holograms;
15 photographs;	8 pictures;	50 post cards;
10 stereographs;	12 study prints;	

When the entry is for a multi-set, the number of sets is given, followed by the number of prints in each set or the total of the prints in the sets.

6 sets of study prints: 8 prints each;
6 sets of study prints: 48 prints;

The number of prints in the sets may be omitted from the Collation statement and recorded after the titles of the sets if they are listed in the Contents note.

E. Color Statement. The abbreviation "col." is used for pictures in color, "b&w" for those in black and white, "col. and b&w" for sets containing both color and black and white pictures. If considered necessary, additional color specifics may be given in the Extension of physical description note or in the Summary.

F. Size. Give the height times the width of the mount in centimeters, using the abbreviation "cm." If there is no mount, give the dimensions of the entire sheet on which the picture is printed. For an art original, give the dimensions of the actual picture, excluding margins, etc.

I. Accompaniments. Give the number, if more than one, the specific medium designator, and the physical description of the material that provides the sound for the pictures (see Card 112). The physical description may be omitted (see Card 113).

J. Other Physical Characteristics. Give a brief description of other physical characteristics that may be pertinent to the utilization or storage of the pictures, such as information about the mount, the type and dimensions of the frame, container, etc.

mounted.
unmounted.
in portfolio, 47 x 33 cm.
framed.
wood frame, 51 x 41 cm.

When the information cannot be succinctly stated, the description of these physical properties should be given in a note instead of in the Collation.

SERIES (Area 6)

(Series title; number within the series: Subseries title; number within the subseries)

Apply Basic Rules IX.A,B, p. 20. (see Cards 112, 113).

NOTES (Area 7)

Apply Basic Rules X.A.-I, p. 21. Notes are designed to provide supplementary information about the picture(s) not brought out in the formal description. They should be as brief as clarity and good grammar permit, and may be combined and grouped together to create a logical entry. The fullness of detail will vary according to the needs of the particular clientele.

B. Extension of Physical Description. Give any additional information required for a more complete description of the physical properties of the picture(s), such as the medium, technique, color specifics, unusual framing or mounting, etc.

Acrylic painting.
Charcoal and ink drawing.
Lithograph.
Silk scroll attached to rods.
Portraits in sepia.
An abstract painting in yellow and blue.
Tinted photographs.
An English landscape depicted in pastel colors.

C. Accompanying and/or Descriptive Material. Briefly describe material designed to assist in the understanding of the picture(s) (see Cards 108-113).

Text on verso of prints.
Captions and biographical notes in lower margins.
With teacher's guide.
Notes on inside covers of portfolio.

D. Other Versions. For an art print give the medium of the original work, the date of execution, and its present location, if known (see Card 108).

H. Summary. If an art original is known to be housed in an institution or collection, this information is included in the Summary (see Cards 108-111).

I. Contents. Record the titles of pictures in a set if they are distinctive (see Card 112). Sets often contain so many pictures that a listing of all the titles is impractical. In such cases, a Partial Contents note may suffice, or the Contents note may be omitted in favor of a Summary that adequately covers the subjects involved. In a multi-set entry note the titles of the sets are followed by the number of pictures in each set if the number has not been recorded in the Collation. The caption "CONTENTS" or "PARTIAL CONTENTS" may be omitted.

OTHER IDENTIFYING AND ORGANIZATIONAL DATA (Area 8)

Apply Basic Rules XI.A-E, p. 24.

D. Media Code. All pictures may be coded under the general designator coding for pictures "PA", or each format may be coded separately under the coding for its specific designator.

Art original	PO	Post card	PC
Art print	PR	Poster	PT
Hologram	PH	Stereograph	PG
Photograph	PP	Study print	PS
Picture	PI		

```
PA
759.4   Renoir, Pierre Auguste
REN        Portrait of a young girl.  [Picture]  Green-
        wich, CT: New York Graphic Society, [197-?]
           1 art print: col; 61 x 51 cm; framed.
           Reproduction of his painting in oil, 1888.
           Original in the Museum of Art, São Paulo.

        PAINTINGS, FRENCH/ PAINTINGS, MODERN- 19TH
        CENTURY/ PORTRAITS/ t
```

CARD 108
Art print.
Creator main entry.
General medium code in call number.
Notes:
Other versions.
Summary.

```
PP
977     The Dust Bowl.  [Picture]  Mt. Dora, FL: Docu-
DUS        mentary Photo Aids, [196-]
           30 photographs: b&w; 28 x 36 cm.
           With teacher's guide.
           Depicts the ravages of the dust storms in
        the Midwest in the 1930's and how the people
        were affected.

        MIDDLE WEST/ U.S.- ECONOMIC CONDITIONS
```

CARD 109
Photograph set.
Set title main entry.
Specific medium code in call number.
Summary (caption omitted).

```
301.45  Black America yesterday and today.  [Picture]
BLA        Elgin, IL: David C. Cook, c1969.
           20 pictures: col; 28 x 36 cm.  K-J.
           With resource booklet by Helen Ward Carry
        and Levi Lathen.
           Presents Negro history and biography.


        NEGROES- BIOGRAPHY/ NEGROES- HISTORY

                                               PA:PI
```

CARD 110
Picture set.
Set title main entry.
Educational level note.
Medium code at bottom of card.
Summary (caption omitted).

```
920     Founders of American freedom.  [Picture]
FOU        Pasadena, CA: Audio Visual Enterprises, c1962.
           8 study prints: col; 28 x 36 cm.
           Text on verso of prints.
           SUMMARY: Presents portraits and contributions
        of Franklin, Washington, Samuel Adams, John
        Adams, Jefferson, Madison, Hamilton, and Mar-
        shall.

        U.S.- BIOGRAPHY- PORTRAITS
```

CARD 111
Study print set.
Set title main entry.

598.2 Common birds, group 1. [Picture] Chicago: So-
COM-1 ciety for Visual Education, c1963.
8 study prints: col; 34 x 47 cm. & audiodisc: 12 in; 33.3 rpm. (Basic science series 100; no. 4) Primary.
Teaching guide and text on verso of prints.
CONTENTS: Great horned owl.- Cardinal.- Blue jay.- Redwing blackbird.- Mourning dove.- Brown thrasher.- Robin.- Hairy woodpecker.

BIRDS/ ser

CARD 112
Study print set.
Set title main entry.
Audio accompaniment.
Series statement.
Educational level note.
Contents note.

598.2 Common birds, group 1. Picture. SVE, 1963.
COM-1 8 study prints: col; 34 x 47 cm. & audiodisc. (Basic science series 100) P.
Teaching guide and text on verso of prints.

BIRDS

CARD 113
Study print set.
Set title main entry.
Simplified cataloging.
Medium designator without brackets.

Medium Designator: **REALIA**

Specific Designators:
Name of object
Specimen

Description

Realia are real things as they are, without alteration. Realia inclclude both natural objects and those produced by human workmanship. Replicas of natural objects and of handcrafted or machine-made things that are of historical or artistic significance (e.g., artifacts, original sculptures) are not considered realia and are cataloged as models (see p. 144). A *specimen* is a part or aspect of some item that is a typical sample of the character of others in its same class or group.

MAIN ENTRY (Area 1)

Apply Basic Rules IV.A-C, p. 4.

A. Title Main Entry. Title main entry is preferred.

B. Series Title Main Entry. When realia are issued in sets they are usually entered under the title of the set (see Cards 114, 117). When single items or sets of realia are issued in a series, main entry under series title may be made in accordance with Basic Rules IV.B1-3 (see Card 115).

C. Creator Main Entry. An original three-dimensional work of art is entered under the name of the artist (see Card 116).

TITLE/MEDIUM DESIGNATOR/STATEMENT OF CREATOR RESPONSIBILITY (Area 2)

A. Title. Follow Basic Rules V.A1-10, p. 7, as applicable. The title is taken from the container in which the realia are stored, or from accompanying data. Preference is given the title on accompanying material if variation occurs. If no title is found in these or other sources, a descriptive title is supplied by the cataloger and is shown in brackets (see Card 115).

B. Medium Designator. Apply Basic Rule V.B1, p. 10. The general physical form designator (medium designator) "Realia", which is in the plural form, is given following the Title statement and is usually enclosed in square brackets. The brackets may be omitted.

C. Statement of Creator Responsibility. In general, no statement of creator responsibility can be given for realia. In a few instances, persons such as scientists, archeologists, artists, inventors, etc., who are responsible for discovering or collecting natural or historical realia, or designing hand-made or machine-made articles, may be cited in accordance with Basic Rule V.C, p. 13.

EDITION (Area 3)

Not applicable. Realia are usually not available in different "editions".

IMPRINT (Area 4)

Apply Basic Rules VII.A-C, p. 15, where appropriate. The customary connotation associated with the data in the Imprint statement usually does not apply to realia.

A. Place. Since realia often do not have a "producer", the location where the item was discovered may be recorded in "place" position in the Imprint statement; or, place may be omitted from the Imprint and be given in a note. If a notation is required in Imprint position (e.g., for computer programming) the abbreviation "[s.l.]" may be used.

B. Producer/Sponsor/Distributor. The organization or commercial firm that collects, packages, and/or manufactures specimens or other realia specifically for distribution is regarded as the producer, sponsor, or distributor in accordance with the function performed, and is named in the Imprint. For other realia (e.g., natural objects) a producer/sponsor/distributor is inappropriate. If a notation is required in Imprint position (e.g., for computer programming) the abbreviation "[s.n.]" may be used.

C. Date. Give a known or conjectured date. The date may be that of origin, discovery, collection, or distribution. If necessary, the significance of the date may be explained in a note.

COLLATION (PHYSICAL DESCRIPTION) (Area 5)*

Number and name of/object(s)/specimen(s): description of color, size, container, and other physical characteristics, as appropriate.

The elements described and the terminology used in the Collation statement will vary in accordance with the wide diversity of physical characteristics of realia.

---

*The first statement under Collation, and Series, shows all the elements in each area as they would be recorded on the catalog card.

A. Number of Items and Specific Designator. State the number of items together with the name(s) of the object(s) and specimen(s). In many instances, this identification may be the only element in the Collation statement.

3 hand puppets — 5 artifacts
1 porcelain bowl — 10 rock specimens
1 Indian feather headband, 1 pair beaded moccasins

When the entry is for a multi-set, the number of sets is given, followed by the number of items in each set or the total of the items in the sets.

5 sets of mineral specimens: 10 specimens each
5 sets of mineral specimens: 50 specimens

The number of items in the sets may be omitted from the Collation statement and recorded after the titles of the sets if they are listed in the Contents note.

E., F., J. Various Other Applicable Elements. Color, size, container, and other physical characteristics may be described as separate elements in the usual pattern, or be combined in a brief continuous statement. The color statement may be general (col.) or specific (blue and yellow). Dimensions are given in centimeters. This physical description may be entirely omitted from the Collation when it can be better stated in a note.

SERIES (Area 6)

(Series title; number within the series: Subseries title; number within the subseries)

Apply Basic Rules IX.A,B, p. 20. (See Card 114).

NOTES (Area 7)

Apply Basic Rules X.A-I, p. 21. For realia, a summary which combines the supplementary information often given in several separate notes, may provide a sufficiently clear and brief description.

OTHER IDENTIFYING AND ORGANIZATIONAL DATA (Area 8)

Apply Basic Rules XI.A-E, p. 24.

D. Media Code. All realia may be coded under the general designator coding for realia "RA". Specimens may be coded separately under the specific designator coding "RS". When the name of the object is used as the specific designator the coding is "RO".

RA
791.5 Hand puppets. [Realia] Circle Pines, MN:
HAN American Guidance Service, 1971.
6 puppets: col; 30 cm. long; cloth. (Duso kit D-1) K-P.
SUMMARY: The puppets, designed to dramatize real-life situations, include one adult male, one adult female, two male children, and two female children.

PUPPETS AND PUPPET PLAYS/ ser

CARD 114
Set of realia.
Set title main entry.
General medium code in call number.
Series statement.
Educational level note.
Summary.

RA
791.5 Hand puppets: [Boy puppets] [Realia] Circle
HAN Pines, MN: American Guidance Service, 1971.
2 puppets: col; 30 cm. long; cloth. (Duso kit D-1) K-P.
SUMMARY: Puppets from a set designed to dramatize real-life situations.

PUPPETS AND PUPPET PLAYS/ t: Boy puppets./ ser

CARD 115
Realia: part of a set cataloged separately.
Set title main entry; supplied individual title treated as a subtitle.

```
735     Boccioni, Umberto
GOC        Muscular dynamism, or, Unique forms of con-
        tinuity in space.  [Realia]  1913.
           1 sculpture: polished bronze; 110 cm. high.
           In the Museum of Modern Art, Milan.
           Study of a figure in motion.

        FUTURISM (ART)/ SCULPTURE/ t: Unique forms of
        continuity in space./ t
```

RA:RO

CARD 116
Realia.
Creator main entry.
Alternative title.
Summary (caption omitted).
Medium code at bottom of card.

```
RS
594     Adventure with sea shells.  [Realia]  New York:
ADV        Golden Pr., 1957.
           25 shell specimens: plastic covered; in box
        28 x 38 cm.
           Book entitled The adventure book of shells
        by Eva Knox Evans in container.

        SHELLS/ Evans, Eva Knox.  The adventure book of
        shells./ t: Sea shells.
```

CARD 117
Realia: set of specimens.
Set title main entry.
Specific medium code in call number.

Medium Designator: **SLIDE**

Specific Designators:

Audioslide
Microscope slide
Slide
Stereoscope slide

Description

A *slide* is an image, usually photographic, on film, glass, or other transparent material, designed for projection. Slides are usually mounted in 2 x 2 inch (5 x 5 cm.) cardboard or plastic frames. Glass mounted slides, 3¼ x 4 inches (8 x 10 cm.), are often referred to as lantern slides. An *audioslide* has a magnetically coated mount on which sound is recorded, or one on which a short length of audiotape is attached. An audioslide requires audioslide equipment for projection. A *microscope slide*, usually made of glass, is designed for the examination of an object through a microscope. It may be projected by using a microprojector or a special lens attached to the microscope. In a *stereoscope slide*, a pair of photographic images are mounted to give a three-dimensional effect when viewed through stereoscope equipment.

MAIN ENTRY (Area 1)

Apply Basic Rules IV.A-C, p. 4.

A. Title Main Entry. Title main entry is usually preferred, except for reproductions of works originally entered under the name of the creator (see Creator Main Entry).

B. Series Title Main Entry. When slides are issued in sets they are usually entered under the title of the set. When one slide in the set is cataloged as a separate entity, its title is treated as a subtitle of the set title.

Individual title:	Robert M. Strozier Library.
Set title:	Florida State University buildings.
Main entry title:	Florida State University buildings: Robert M. Strozier Library.

An added entry is made for the title of the individual slide.

When sets of slides are issued in a series, main entry under series title may be made in accordance with Basic Rules IV.B1-3 (see Card 120).

C. Creator Main Entry. A slide or set of slides that reproduces a work(s) that is entered under the name of a creator is entered in the same manner as the original. For example, a reproduction of a painting is entered under the name of the artist (see Card 119), especially when it is desirable to keep together all formats of a work of an artist. An added entry is made for the title of the slide, and for the title of the original work if it differs from that of the slide.

A compiler of a set of slides is not regarded as a creator. The slides are entered under the title of the set, the compiler may be cited in the Statement of creator responsibility or in a note, and an added entry may be made for his name.

TITLE/MEDIUM DESIGNATOR/STATEMENT OF CREATOR RESPONSIBILITY (Area 2)

A. Title. Apply Basic Rules V.A1-10, p. 7. The title of a single slide is taken from the mount, from accompanying literature, or from the envelope in which it is stored. The title for a set of slides is taken from the container. The same title, or a shortened version of it, may appear on each slide in the set and also in accompanying data. Variations in title, if significant, may be noted. If no title is found for a single slide or a set of slides, one may be supplied by the cataloger and shown in brackets.

B. Medium Designator. Apply Basic Rule V.B1, p. 10. The general physical form designator (medium designator) "Slide" is given in the singular form following the Title statement and is usually enclosed in brackets. The brackets may be omitted (see Card 121).

C. Statement of Creator Responsibility. Apply Basic Rule V.C, p. 13 (see Card 122).

EDITION (Area 3)

Apply Basic Rule VI, p. 14.

IMPRINT (Area 4)*

Place: Producer, copyright/production date; sponsored by Sponsor; Place: Distributed/Released by Distributor, release date.

Apply Basic Rules VII.A-C, p. 15.

---

*The first statement under Imprint, Collation, and Series, shows all the elements in each area as they would be recorded on the catalog card.

COLLATION (PHYSICAL DESCRIPTION) (Area 5)

Number of audioslide(s)/microscope slide(s)/slide(s)/stereoscope slide(s): color/black and white; height x width in inches or centimeters & audio accompaniment(s); other physical characteristics.

A. Number of Items and Specific Designator

5 audioslides: 9 microscope slides: 1 slide:
80 slides: 21 stereoscope slides:

3 sets of slides: 20 slides each;
3 sets of slides: 60 slides;

When the entry is for a multi-set, the number of sets is given, followed by the number of slides in each set (see Card 120) or the total of the slides in the sets. The number of slides in the sets may be omitted from the Collation statement and recorded after the titles of the sets if they are listed in the Contents note.

When slides (except microscope slides) are not made of film, note the composition of the material, in parentheses, after the specific medium designator (see Card 119).

40 slides (glass):

When microscope slides are not made of glass, note the composition of the material, in parentheses, after the specific medium designator.

12 microscope slides (plastic):

E. Color Statement. The abbreviation "col." is used for slides in color, "b&w" for those in black and white, "col. and b&w" for sets containing both color and black and white slides.

A color statement is not given for microscope slides. If the slides are stained, this fact is noted in lieu of the color statement.

12 microscope slides (plastic): stained;

F. Size. Give the height times the width of the mount in inches or centimeters, using the abbreviation "in." or "cm." If there is no mount, as in microscope slides, the dimensions of the entire transparent surface are given. Metric measurement is preferred, but until the conversion is well understood, the size of slides may be shown in inches. The metric measurements for the most commonly used slide sizes are:

1 x 3 in. – 3 x 8 cm. 2 x 2 in. – 5 x 5 cm. 3¼ x 4 in. – 8 x 10 cm.

I. Accompaniments. Give the number, if more than one, the specific medium designator, and the physical description (see Audiorecording) of the material that provides the sound for the slides (see Card 122). The physical description may be omitted (see Card 118). The tape on an audioslide is not regarded as a separate audio accompaniment.

J. Other Physical Characteristics. Give a brief description of other physical characteristics that may be pertinent to the utilization or storage of the slides, such as the type of container, kind of mount, etc.

in plastic sleeve in folder.
in transparent pages in loose-leaf binder.
in 3 Kodak Carousel trays.
plastic mount.

When the information cannot be succinctly stated, the description of these physical properties should be given in a note instead of in the Collation.

SERIES (Area 6)

(Series title; number within the series: Subseries title: number within the subseries)

Apply Basic Rules IX.A,B, p. 20. (See Card 119).

NOTES (Area 7)

Apply Basic Rules X.A-I, p. 21. Notes are designed to provide supplementary information about the slide(s) not brought out in the formal description. They should be as brief as clarity and good grammar permit, and may be combined and grouped together to create a logical entry. The fullness of detail will vary according to the needs of the particular clientele.

B. Extension of Physical Description. Give any additional information required to convey a more complete picture of the physical properties of the work, or of special equipment needed to project the slides (see Card 124).

Requires Sound-on-slide projector.
May be projected with microscope projector.

C. Accompanying and/or Descriptive Material. Briefly describe material designed to assist in the understanding of the slide(s) (see Cards 118-122, 124).

Teacher's guide in binder.
Captions.
Text on mounts.
Notes on inside of folder.
Notes on envelope of each slide.

D. Other Versions. When a slide is a representation of a work of art, give the medium of the original work, the date of execution, and its present location, if known (see Card 119).

Reproduction of the artist's painting in oil, 1955.
Original in the National Gallery of Art, Washington, D.C.

I. Contents. Record the titles of slides in a set if they are distinctive. Sets often contain so many slides that a listing of all the titles is impractical. In such cases, a Partial Contents note may suffice, or the Contents note may be omitted in favor of a Summary that adequately covers the subjects involved. In a multi-set entry note the titles of the sets (see Cards 120, 124), followed by the number of slides in each set if the number has not been recorded in the Collation. The caption "CONTENTS" or "PARTIAL CONTENTS" may be omitted (see Card 124).

OTHER IDENTIFYING AND ORGANIZATIONAL DATA (Area 8)

Apply Basic Rules XI.A-E, p. 24.

D. Media Code. All slides may be coded under the general designator coding for slides "SA", or each format may be coded separately under the coding for its specific designator.

Audioslide	SO
Microscope slide	SM
Slide	SL
Stereoscope slide	SS

SA
301.6 No man is an island: an inquiry into alienation.
NOM [Slide] White Plains, NY: Center for Humanities, c1972.

160 slides: col; 2 x 2 in. & 2 audiocassettes and discs; in 2 Kodak carousels. H-A.

With teacher's guide.

SUMMARY: A portrayal of the alienation of humanity using such personalities as Van Gogh, St. Francis, Tom Paine, and Hemingway, to produce an inquiry-oriented study.

ALIENATION (SOCIAL PSYCHOLOGY)

CARD 118
Slide set.
Set title main entry.
General medium code in call number.
Audio accompaniment.

Notes:
Educational level.
Accompanying and/or descriptive material.
Summary.

SL
759.5 Leonardo da Vinci
LEO Mona Lisa. [Slide] Stamford, CT: Sandak, [1972?]

1 slide (glass): col; 2 x 2 in. (5 x 5 cm.); plastic mount. (Masterpieces from the Louvre)

Notes on mount.

Reproduction of his painting in oil, 1503-06.

Original in the Louvre Museum, Paris.

PAINTINGS, ITALIAN/ t/ ser

CARD 119
Slide.
Creator main entry.
Specific medium code in call number.
Metric conversion.
Series statement.

Notes:
Accompanying and/or descriptive material.
Other versions.

709.51 The Art of China. [Slide] Great Neck, NY: Edu-
ART cational Dimensions Corp., c1972.
3 sets of slides: 20 slides each; col; 2 x 2
in; in plastic pages.
With lecture notes for each set.
CONTENTS: Painting.- Ceramics.- Sculpture.

ART, CHINESE

CARD 120
Slide sets.
Series title main entry.
Contents note.

709.51 The Art of China. No. 1, Painting. Slide.
ART-1 Educational Dimensions, c1972.
20 slides: col; 2 x 2 in.
Lecture notes.

PAINTING, CHINESE

CARD 121
One slide set from a multi-set.
Series title main entry.
Simplified cataloging.
Medium designator without brackets.

```
913.32  Tutenkhamen's treasures.  [Slide]  Photographs
TUT        by Harry Burton; lecture from reports by
           Howard Carter.  The Metropolitan Museum of
           Art and Macmillan Co., c1972.
           40 slides: col. and b&w; 2 x 2 in. & 1 audio-
        disc: 12 in; 33.3 rpm.
           With 4 teacher's guides.
           An account of Howard Carter's discovery of
        the tomb which serves as an introduction to the
        field of Egyptology.
        ARCHEOLOGY/ EGYPT- ANTIQUITIES/ Burton, Harry/
        Carter, Howard
```

CARD 122
Slide set.
Set title main entry.
Statement of creator responsibility.
Joint producers.
Audio accompaniment.
Summary (caption omitted).
Creator added entries.

```
599     Tooth development.  [Slide]  Carolina Biological
TOO        Supply Co., [197-?]
           9 microscope slides: 3 x 8 cm.
           Sections of fetal pig mandibles show tooth
        development in nine successive stages.



        PIGS- ANATOMY


                                                 SA:SM
```

CARD 123
Microscope slide set.
Set title main entry.
Medium code at bottom of card.
Metric measurement.
Place omitted.
Summary (caption omitted).

```
398.8   Mother Goose rhymes.  [Slide]  New York: GAF
MOT        Corp., [197-?]
           21 stereoscope slides: col; in 3 circular
        cardboard reels, 9 cm. & 1 audiodisc, 8 cm;
        attached to reel.
           View-Master, AVB 410.
           Captions on reels.
           Little Miss Muffet; Little Boy Blue; Peter,
        Peter, pumpkin-eater.- Little Bo-Peep; Three
        little kittens; Jack and Jill.- Hey, diddle,
        diddle; There was a crooked man; Humpty Dumpty
        sat on a wall;          Mary had a little lamb.
        NURSERY RHYMES/     O     Mother Goose
```

CARD 124
Stereoscope slide set.
Set title main entry.
Notes:
Extension of physical description.
Accompanying and/or descriptive material.
Contents (caption omitted).

Medium Designator: **TRANSPARENCY**

Specific Designator:
Transparency

Description

A *transparency* is an image on transparent material designed to be used with an overhead projector or light box. All transparencies attached on all four sides to the under surface of the mount constitute the "basic" transparency. A transparency hinged on one side on the upper surface of the mount and designed to be laid over the "basic" transparency is called an overlay.

MAIN ENTRY (Area 1)

Apply Basic Rules IV.A-C, p. 4.

A. Title Main Entry. Title main entry is preferred for transparencies since they are usually identified by title by the producer and the user.

B. Series Title Main Entry. When transparencies are issued in sets they are usually entered under the title of the set. When one transparency in the set is cataloged as a separate entity, its title is treated as a subtitle of the set title (see Card 128). When sets of transparencies are issued in a series, main entry under series title may be made in accordance with Basic Rules IV.B1-3 (see Card 129).

C. Creator Main Entry. A transparency that reproduces a work (e.g., a painting) or a part of a work (e.g., tables from a book) that is entered under the name of the creator may be entered in the same manner as the original. An added entry is made for the title of the transparency, and for the title of the original work if it differs from that of the transparency.

TITLE/MEDIUM DESIGNATOR/STATEMENT OF CREATOR RESPONSIBILITY (Area 2)

A. Title. Apply Basic Rules V.A1-10, p. 7. The title is taken from the transparency itself, from its mount, accompanying data, file folder, or container in which it is stored. If no title is found, one may be supplied by the cataloger and shown in brackets.

B. Medium Designator. Apply Basic Rule V.B1, p. 10. The general physical form designator (medium designator) "Transparency" is given in the singular form following the Title statement and is usually enclosed in square brackets. The brackets may be omitted (see Card 126).

C. Statement of Creator Responsibility. Apply Basic Rule V.C, p. 13 (see Card 130).

EDITION (Area 3)

Apply Basic Rule VI, p. 14 (see Cards 127, 130).

IMPRINT (Area 4)*

Place: Producer, copyright/production date; sponsored by Sponsor; Place: Distributed/Released by Distributor, release date.

Apply Basic Rules VII.A-C, p. 15.

COLLATION (PHYSICAL DESCRIPTION) (Area 5)

Number of transparency(ies); number of overlay(s); color/black and white; height x width in centimeters & integral accompaniment(s); other physical characteristics.

A. Number of Items and Specific Designator

1 transparency: 36 transparencies:

3 sets of transparencies: 6 transparencies each;
3 sets of transparencies: 18 transparencies;

When the entry is for a multi-set, the number of sets is given, followed by the number of transparencies in each set or the total of the transparencies in the sets. The number of transparencies in the sets may be omitted from the Collation statement and recorded after the titles of the sets if they are listed in the Contents note (see Card 129).

In simplified cataloging, if the entry describes only one transparency, the number and the specific designator "transparency" may be omitted since it is the same as the general designator (see Card 126).

---

*The first statement under Imprint, Collation, and Series, shows all the elements in each area as they would be recorded on the catalog cards.

B. Physical Contents. The presence of overlays and their number, if readily ascertainable and significant, is given.

1 transparency: 4 overlays;
32 transparencies: overlays;
3 sets of transparencies: 6 transparencies each, overlays;

E. Color Statement. The abbreviation "col." is used for transparencies in color, "b&w" for those in black and white.

F. Size. Give the height times the width of the mount in centimeters, using the abbreviation "cm." If there is no mount, the dimensions of the entire transparent surface are given. The metric measurements for some of the most commonly used transparency mounts are:

8 x 10 in. . . . . 20 x 25 cm.
10 x 12 in. . . . . 25 x 30 cm.
9 x 11 in. . . . . 23 x 28 cm.
11 x 12 in. . . . . 28 x 30 cm.

I. Accompaniments. In some instances, transparencies are designed to be used with an accompaniment, such as a special type of mount or an audiorecording. This accompaniment is considered an integral part of the transparency and its description, preceded by "&", is given after the dimensions (see Card 129).

J. Other Physical Characteristics. Give a brief description of other physical characteristics that may be pertinent to the utilization or storage of the transparencies, such as the type and dimensions of the container, peculiarities of the mount, etc.

in carrying case, 33 x 36 x 13 cm.
plastic mount.
without mount.
in file folders.

When the information cannot be succinctly stated, the description of these physical properties should be given in a note instead of in the Collation.

SERIES (Area 6)

(Series title; number within the series: Subseries title; number within the subseries)

Apply Basic Rules IX.A,B, p. 20. (See Cards 125, 126, 130).

NOTES (Area 7)

Apply Basic Rules X.A-I, p. 21. Notes are designed to provide supplementary information about the transparency not brought out in the formal description. They should be as brief as clarity and good grammar permit, and may be combined and grouped together to create a logical entry. The fullness of detail will vary according to the needs of the particular clientele.

B. Extension of Physical Description. Give any additional information required to convey a more complete picture of the physical properties of the work, or of special equipment needed to project the transparencies (see Card 128).

Use with Flipatran viewing stage.
Requires polarized spinner.
May be projected onto a chalkboard.

I. Contents. Record the titles of transparencies in a set if they are distinctive. Sets often contain so many transparencies that a listing of all the titles is impractical. In such cases, a Partial Contents note may suffice, or the Contents note may be omitted in favor of a summary that adequately covers the subjects involved. In a multi-set entry note the titles of the sets, followed by the number of transparencies in each set if the number has not been recorded in the Collation (see Card 129). The caption "CONTENTS" or "PARTIAL CONTENTS" may be omitted.

OTHER IDENTIFYING AND ORGANIZATIONAL DATA (Area 8)

Apply Basic Rules XI.A-E, p. 24.

D. Media Code. All transparencies may be coded under the general designator coding for transparencies "TA", or under the specific designator coding "TR". Should new distinctive formats of transparencies be developed, additional specific designators and codings may be added.

```
TA
910     World races.  [Transparency]  Chicago: Denoyer-
WOR-7      Geppert, 1968.
           1 transparency: col; 20 x 25 cm.  (World
        geography; no. 7)  J-H.
           SUMMARY: Shows the distribution of Caucasoid,
        Mongoloid, Negroid and Indo-Australoid peoples
        of the world.


        ETHNOLOGY/ ser
```

CARD 125
Transparency.
Title main entry.
General medium code in call number.
Series statement.
Notes:
Educational level. Summary.

```
910     World races.  Transparency.  Denoyer, 1968.
WOR-7      col; 20 x 25 cm.  (World geography)
           Shows the distribution of Caucasoid, Mongo-
        loid, Negroid and Indo-Australoid peoples of
        the world.



        ETHNOLOGY/ ser

                                               TA:TR
```

CARD 126
Transparency.
Title main entry.
Simplified cataloging.
Medium code at bottom of card.
Medium designator without brackets.

TR
612.6 The Wonder of new life. Unit 2. [Transparency]
WON-2 Cleveland Health Museum; distributed by Cleveland Health Museum and Education Center, c1971.

6 transparencies: 7 overlays; col; 28 x 30 cm.

With teachers' guides and script. Captions.

Revised version of the 1968 set entitled EMT transparencies.

Presents the processes of menstruation and the development of the human embryo. Supplements the set Wonder of new life. Unit 1.

EMBRYOLOGY/ MENSTRUATION/ t: EMT transparencies.

CARD 127
Transparency set.
Set title main entry.
Specific medium code in call number.
Place omitted.
Distributor.

Notes:
Accompanying and/or descriptive material.
Edition.
Summary (caption omitted).

909 World history map transparencies. No. 32, In-
WOR-32 dustrial agrarian-commercial world. [Transparency] Chicago: Denoyer-Geppert, c1968.

1 transparency: col; 20 x 25 cm.

Use with Flipatran viewing stage.

Highlights the inset on the correlated world history map entitled World relationships, July 1, 1967.

INDUSTRY- HISTORY- MAPS/ t: World relationships, July 1, 1967./ t: Industrial ... world.

CARD 128
One transparency from a set.
Set title main entry.

Notes:
Extension of physical description.
Related works.

530.07 PRO The Project physics course. [Transparency] New York: Holt, c1970.
6 sets of transparencies: col; 20 x 25 cm. & Visu-book stage.
Correlated with the textbook of the same title.
CONTENTS: Concepts of motion, 11 transparencies.- Motion in the heavens, 6 transparencies.- The triumph of mechanics, 11 transparencies.- Light and electromagnetism, 5 transparencies.- Models of the atom, 5 transparencies.- The nucleus, 9 transparencies.

PHYSICS- STUDY  AND TEACHING

CARD 129
Transparency sets.
Series title main entry.
Accompaniment.

Notes:
Related works.
Contents.

421 REC Recognizing long and short vowel sounds. [Transparency] Author, Leon Weisman. Rev. ed. Big Spring, TX: Creative Visuals, c1967.
12 transparencies: col; 30 cm. circle. (Reading skills) Primary.
With teacher's manual.

PHONETICS/ VOWELS/ ser

CARD 130
Transparency set.
Set title main entry.
Statement of creator responsibility.
Edition statement.
Circular shape dimension.
Series statement.

Notes:
Educational level.
Accompanying and/or descriptive material.

Medium Designator: VIDEORECORDING

Specific Designators:
Cartridge
Cassette
Disc
Reel

Description

A *videorecording* is a transcription of audio and/or video signals designed for playback on television equipment. Magnetic tape is the most commonly used material for recording the signals. Tapes are produced in different widths (2, 1, ¾, ½, ¼ inches) and formats (cartridge, cassette, reel) for playback at various speeds. A *cartridge* contains a tape which has the ends spliced together to form a loop and run continuously. A *cassette* is a reel-to-reel tape enclosed in a cassette. A *reel* tape is wound on an open reel and runs from reel to reel. The signals may also be recorded on a *disc*. Videorecordings on discs and on other materials, such as film and magnetized plastic sheets, are currently in various stages of development and testing and production on a large scale is anticipated.

MAIN ENTRY (Area 1)

Apply Basic Rules IV.A-C, p. 4.

A. Title Main Entry. As a general rule, videorecordings are entered under title since they are usually identified by title, and the extent of collaborative contribution makes it difficult to attribute to one person or corporate body the overall responsibility for the creation of the work.

B. Series Title Main Entry. When videorecordings are issued in series or sets, each is usually cataloged under its own title, and an added entry is made for the series title. The series title may be used for main entry when the title of the individual videorecording is dependent upon the series title for meaning (see Cards 131, 133), or when the title of the individual videorecording is dependent upon the series title for meaning (see Cards 131, 133), or when the individual recording is not available as a separate work because it is sold only as part of a complete set. When the series title becomes the main entry title, the title of each individual unit or set is treated as a subtitle of the series title, and an added entry is made for the title of the individual videorecording or set if it is sufficiently meaningful to stand alone (see Card 134).

When several videorecordings are entered *collectively* under the series title, the titles of the individual recordings are given in a Contents note (see Cards 131, 131A, 134), and added entries are made for them if they are distinctive.

C. Creator Main Entry. A videorecording is rarely entered under the name of a creator because of the difficulty in establishing a creativity priority among the many functions that must be performed in a television production. If, however, the major portion of the intellectual and artistic content is clearly the work of a person *whose name is significant in identifying the videorecording,* creator main entry may be used, and an added entry is made for the title.

The television version of a written work is not usually entered under the author of the original work since it is extremely doubtful that the videorecording is an exact reproduction of the original. Title main entry is used, and an author or author-title added entry is made for the work on which the videorecording is based (see Cards 135, 135A). Some media centers may elect to enter the television version of a written work under the author if learning objectives are better accomplished by keeping together all formats and interpretations of an author's works.

TITLE/MEDIUM DESIGNATOR/STATEMENT OF CREATOR RESPONSIBILITY (Area 2)

A. Title. Apply Basic Rules V.A1-10, p.7. The title is taken from the videorecording itself. In some instances, the title is given only orally and does not appear in written form. If the videorecording does not provide adequate information, the title is taken from the cartridge, cassette, or disc, from accompanying material, producer's catalog, or label on the container. If no title is found, one is supplied by the cataloger and shown in brackets.

If more than one title appears on the videorecording, preference is given the title closest to the subject content. Significant title variations are cited in a note, and added entries may be made for variant titles by which the work may be known.

B. Medium Designator. Apply Basic Rule V.B1, p. 10. The general physical form designator (medium designator) "Videorecording" is given in the singular form following the Title statement and is usually enclosed in square brackets. The brackets may be omitted.

C. Statement of Creator Responsibility. Apply Basic Rule V.C, p. 13. The function(s) performed and the name(s) of the creator(s) are stated after the medium designator *if they are significant in identifying the work,* such as those of well-known producers and directors, and added entries are made for these names, as appropriate (see Cards 131, 131A, 133, 134).

EDITION (Area 3)

Apply Basic Rule VI, p. 14.

IMPRINT (Area 4)*

Place: Producer, copyright/production date; sponsored by Sponsor; Place: Distributed/Released by Distributor, release date.

Apply Basic Rules VII.A-C, p. 15.

C. Date. In the absence of a copyright, production, or release date, the date of the first broadcast, if known, may be used and identified as such in a note, e.g., Telecast in 1974.

COLLATION (PHYSICAL DESCRIPTION) (Area 5)

Number of cartridge(s)/cassette(s)/disc(s),/reel(s),/diameter of disc(s)/reel(s): number of minutes; silent/sound; color/black and white; tape/film width; other physical characteristics.

A. Number of Items and Specific Designator

3 cartridges: 2 cassettes: 1 cassette (film):

When a cartridge, cassette, or reel videorecording is not on tape, note the material (e.g., film) on which the signals are recorded, in parentheses, after the specific medium designator (see Card 136).

2 reels, 7 in. (18 cm.): 1 disc, 9 in. (23 cm.):

Give the diameter of reels and discs following the specific designator. Metric measurement is preferred, but until the conversion is well understood, the diameter may be shown in inches, followed, if desired, by the centimeter measurement in parentheses (see Card 135). If the diameter of the reel is not considered important for playback or storage purposes, it may be omitted (see Cards 133, 134).

Give the dimensions of cassettes and cartridges if other than U-Matic, which is the current standard size.

C. Length. Give time duration in minutes using the abbreviation "min." When long videorecordings are divided and mounted separately, give the total running time. When the entry includes two or more recordings, each with the same time duration, give the running time of each (see Cards 131, 133). When the entry includes videorecordings with individual titles, give the running time of each if there are only two, e.g., 25, 30 min.; or the span of time if there are more than two, e.g., 20-30 min.; or omit the time in the Collation and include it after each title in the Contents note.

*The first statement under Imprint, Collation, and Series, shows all the elements in each area as they would be recorded on the catalog card.

D. Sound Statement. The abbreviation "si." is used for silent videorecordings, "sd." for those with sound. Since most videorecordings are sound, the sound statement is frequently omitted (see Cards 132, 134) except for silent videorecordings.

E. Color Statement. The abbreviation "col." is used for color videorecordings, "b&w" for works in black and white.

F. Size. Give the width of tape and film in metric measurement using the abbreviation "mm" (see Card 136). Until the conversion to metric measurement is well understood, the width of tapes may be shown in inches, using the abbreviation "in.", and may be followed, if desired, by the millimeter equivalent in parentheses (see Card 135).

G., H., J. Various Other Applicable Elements. Playback speed, recording mode, and other physical characteristics which can be briefly described, may be noted if they are considered pertinent to the utilization or storage of the work. Playback speed need be stated only if the equipment specified in the Extension of physical description note can run at more than one speed. The playback speed of tapes is given in inches per second, abbreviated to "ips." (e.g., 7.5 ips.), or in centimeters per second (e.g., 19 cmps.); of discs, in revolutions per minute, abbreviated to "rpm." (e.g., 1500 rpm.). Recording mode is identified only if it is other than helical (e.g., quadruplex). If there is more than one sound track, the number is noted.

SERIES (Area 6)

(Series title; number within the series: Subseries title; number within the subseries)

Apply Basic Rules IX.A,B, p. 20 (See Card 135).

NOTES (Area 7)

Apply Basic Rules X.A-I, p. 21. Notes are designed to provide supplementary information about the videorecording not brought out in the formal description. They should be as brief as clarity and good grammar permit, and may be combined or grouped together to create a clear informational and descriptive statement. The fullness of detail will vary according to the needs of the particular clientele.

B. Extension of Physical Description. Indicate the make and model number of the video recorder, and any special equipment or information required for playback (see Cards 131-136). The content of additional audio tracks is also noted.

EIAJ-1. (The standard for ½ in. videotape reel recordings since 1969.)
Sony 3600.
Ampex 7500C. High band.
Motorola EVR Teleplayer.
Spanish language version on second audio track.
Synchronization pulse for slide projector on second audio track.
U-Matic. (The most common ¾ in. videotape cassette since 1972).
Betamax. (A new ½ in. videotape cassette smaller than the U-Matic).

G. Credits. See also Motion Picture: Credits, p. 156.

OTHER IDENTIFYING AND ORGANIZATIONAL DATA (Area 8)

Apply Basic Rules XI.A-E, p. 24.

C. Classification Number. Collections of videorecordings may be organized by subject content and classified by the Library of Congress or Dewey Decimal systems. It is frequently desirable to shelve large collections by accession number, with a media code prefix for the various formats.

D. Media Code. All videorecordings may be coded under the general designator coding for videorecordings "VA", or each format may be coded separately under the coding for its specific designator.

Cartridge	VR
Cassette	VC
Disc	VD
Reel	VT

E. Additional Information. Some catalogs may require the inclusion of additional information such as purchase price, rental rate, restrictions on use of copyrighted material, regional or cooperative location, shelf number, etc. The position of this information in the catalog entry is not prescribed, but should be given in an appropriate area, e.g., purchase price and rental rate may be noted at the end of the Imprint area or following the Standard Number (see Basic Rule XI.A, p. 24).

VA
973
AME

America. [Videorecording] Producer, Michael Gill; writer and narrator, Alistair Cooke. London: BBC-TV; New York: Released by Time-Life Multimedia, 1972.

13 cartridges: 52 min. each; sd; col; 1/2 in. Panasonic NV-5110.

With book by James Shenton.

Also issued in videocassette and 16mm film.

CONTENTS: 1. The new found land.- 2. Home away from home.- 3. Making a revolution.- 4. Inventing a nation.- 5. Gone west.- 6. A fireball

(See next card)

CARD 131
Videorecording, cartridge.
Series title main entry.
General medium code in call number.
Statement of creator responsibility.
Producer/Distributor.
Various notes.

(Card 2)

VA
973
AME

America. [Videorecording]

in the night.- 7. Domesticating a wilderness.- 8. Money on the land.- 9. The huddled masses.- 10. The promise fulfilled and the promise broken.- 11. The arsenal.- 12. First impact.- 13. More abundant life.

U.S.- HISTORY/ Cooke, Alistair

CARD 131A
Continuation card.
Creator added entry.

VC
613.8 Drugs - use or abuse? [Videorecording] Holly-
DRU wood, CA: AIMS Instructional Media Services,
c1972.
1 cassette: 11 min; col; 3/4 in. Intermediate.
Sony VO-1600.
With guide.
16mm motion picture also issued.
Presents basic information about drugs, their nature, use in medicine, and harmful effects when misused.

DRUG ABUSE/ DRUGS

CARD 132
Videorecording, cassette.
Title main entry.
Specific medium code in call number.
Sound notation omitted.
Educational level note.
Summary (caption omitted).

652.3 Typewriting. [Videorecording] Teacher, Guy
TYP Richards. Chicago: TV College, WTTW-TV;
Lincoln, NB: Distributed by Great Plains
National Instructional Television Library,
[197-]
30 reels: 30 min. each; sd; b&w; 2 in; quadruplex.
With study guide.
Issued in a variety of tape formats.
The course is divided into 7 units, each with a different number of lessons that provide practice in basic typing skills.

TYPEWRITING/ Richards, Guy

VA:VT

CARD 133
Videorecording, reel.
Series title main entry.
Medium code at bottom of card.
Statement of creator responsibility.
Summary (caption omitted).
Creator added entry.

```
652.3   Typewriting.  Unit 2, Skill development.
TYP-2      [Videorecording]  Teacher, Guy Richards.
           Chicago: TV College, WTTW-TV; Distributed
           by GPNIT Library, [197-]
           2 reels: 30 min. each; b&w; 2 in; quadruplex.
           With study guide.
           Issued in a variety of tape formats.
           Two lessons from the complete course.
           Skill drills; vertical and horizontal center-
        ing; typing all capitals.- Skill drills; para-
        graph centering; block centering; spread center-
        ing.
        TYPEWRITING/        ○     Richards, Guy/ t: Skill
        development.
```

CARD 134
Videorecording, reel:
one set from a series,
cataloged separately.
Series title main entry:
set title treated
as a subtitle.

Moderately detailed cataloging.
Summary, Contents (captions omitted).

```
616.8   To be or not to be.  [Videorecording]  Ann Arbor,
TOB        MI: Univ. of Michigan Television Center,
           c1969.
           1 reel, 5 in.(13 cm.): 30 min; sd; b&w; 1/2 in.
        (13 mm.)  (Quiet furies; no. 9)
           Shibaden SV-510.
           16mm motion picture also issued.
           Based on the book The quiet furies by Elton
        B. McNeil.
           CREDITS: Producer, Mack Woodruff; directors,
        Marshall Franke, Jack Wellman.

                            ○          (See next card)
```

CARD 135
Videorecording, reel.
Title main entry.
Series statement.
Metric conversion.

Notes:
Related works.
Credits.
Summary.

```
                                                (Card 2)
616.8   To be or not to be.  [Videorecording]
TOB
           SUMMARY: Dramatizes the emotional disorders
        suffered by a homosexual which alters his be-
        havior in everyday life.


        HOMOSEXUALITY/ McNeil, Elton Burbank.  Quiet
        furies./ ser
```

CARD 135A
Continuation card.
Author-title added entry for related work.

```
796.9   The American ski technique.  [Videorecording]
AME        Dayton, OH: Warren Miller Productions, [196-]
           Chicago: Released by Motorola Teleprogram
           Center, 1971.
           1 cassette (film): 15 min; sd; col; 9mm.
           CBS Electronic Video Recording.
           Motorola Teleplayer.
           Demonstrators, Junior Bounous, Sugar Bowl
        staff.
           Covers all phases of the system adopted by
        the Professional Ski Instructors of America.

        SKIS AND SKIING
```

CARD 136
Videorecording, film cassette.
Title main entry.
Probable production date; release date.
Credits, Summary (captions omitted).

APPENDIX I

PHYSICAL DESCRIPTION CHART

Basic elements only are given. For more specific details see the section on the particular medium.

DESIGNATOR	NUMBER OF ITEMS SPECIFIC DESIGNATOR	LENGTH	SOUND	COLOR	SIZE	PLAYBACK SPEED	ACCOMPANIMENTS	OTHER CHARACTERISTICS
Audiorecording	Number of items Specific designator Diameter of disc(s), reel(s) in in./cm.	Duration in min.			Width of tape in in./mm.	Disc: rpm. Tape: ips/ cmps.	Number of items Filmstrip, slide, etc.: specific designator, physical description	Recording mode Width of groove Number of tracks Container description
Chart	Number of items Specific designator			Col./b&w	Height x width in cm.			Mount Cover Material from which chart is made
Diorama	Number of items Specific designator			Col./b&w	Height x width x depth in cm.			Container description, size: h. x w. x. d. in cm.
Filmstrip	Number of items Specific designator	Number of frames		Col./b&w/ col. and b&w	Width of film in mm.		Number of items Audio: specific designator, physical description	Sound synchronization
Flash Card	Number of items Specific designator			Col./b&w	Height x width in cm.		Number of items Audio: specific designator, physical description Manipulative devices: physical description	Mounting, binding, shape, etc. Container description, size: h. x w. x d. in cm.

DESIGNATOR	NUMBER OF ITEMS SPECIFIC DESIGNATOR	LENGTH	SOUND	COLOR	SIZE	PLAYBACK SPEED	ACCOMPANIMENTS	OTHER CHARACTERISTICS
Game	Number of items Specific designator							Physical contents: number, names, description of pieces/various pieces Container description, size: h. x w. x d. in cm.
Globe	Number of items Specific designator			Col./b&w	Diameter in cm.			Mounting Surface Meridians Height in cm.
Kit	Number of items Specific designator							Physical contents: number, names, description of components Container description, size: h. x w. x d. in cm.
Machine-Readable Data File	Number of items Species file specific designator Storage medium specific designator, dimensions	Number of logical records						Labeling information Equipment required Other physical properties of the store
Map	Number of items Specific designator			Col./b&w	Height x width of sheet in cm.			Mount Surface Material from which map is made

DESIGNATOR	NUMBER OF ITEMS SPECIFIC DESIGNATOR	LENGTH	SOUND	COLOR	SIZE	PLAYBACK SPEED	ACCOMPANIMENTS	OTHER CHARACTERISTICS
Microform	Number of items Specific designator			Col./b&w	Cards: h. x w. in cm. Fiche, ultra-fiche: h. x. w. in mm. Film: width in mm.			Negative Container description, size: h. x. w. x d. in cm.
Model	Number of items Specific designator	Physical contents: number, names of pieces/various pieces		Col./specific color	Height x width x depth in cm.			Mounting, etc. Container description, size: h. x w. x d. in cm.
Motion Picture	Number of items Specific designator	Duration in min.	Sd./si.	Col./b&w/ Col. and b&w	Width of film in mm. Indicate super 8mm.			
Picture	Number of items Specific designator Number of sets Specific designator Number of items in sets			Col./b&w	Height x width of mount or of unmounted sheet in cm.		Number of items Audio: specific designator, physical description	Mount, frame, container description, size in cm.

DESIGNATOR	NUMBER OF ITEMS SPECIFIC DESIGNATOR	LENGTH	SOUND	COLOR	SIZE	PLAYBACK SPEED	ACCOMPANIMENTS	OTHER CHARACTERISTICS
Realia	Number of items Specific designator Number of sets Specific designator Number of items in sets			Col./specific color	Appropriate dimensions in cm.			Other physical characteristics Container description, size: h. x w. x d. in cm.
Slide	Number of items Specific designator Number of sets Specific designator Number of items in sets			Col./b&w/ col. and b&w Stained	Height x width of mount or of unmounted slide in in./cm.		Number of items Audio: specific designator, physical description	Mount Container description
Transparency	Number of items Specific designator Number of sets Specific designator Number of items in sets Number of overlays			Col./b&w	Height x width of mount or of unmounted transparency in cm.		Number of items Audio: specific designator, physical description	Mount Container description, size: h. x w. x d. in cm.
Videorecording	Number of items Specific designator Diameter of disc(s), reel(s) in in./cm.	Duration in min.	Sd./si.	Col./b&w	Width of tape, film in in./mm.	Disc: rpm. Tape: ips/cmps.		Recording mode Number of sound tracks

APPENDIX II
GLOSSARY

GENERAL MEDIUM DESIGNATORS are printed in all capital letters, Specific Designators are underlined. Following the definition of the Specific Designator and various other terms, a reference is made to the General Designator or Basic Rule(s) under which a discussion and cataloging examples will be found.

Accession number. The number given to a work in the order of its addition to the collection.

Accompaniments. Works in a medium other than that of the work being cataloged, mechanical devices, or other essential materials that are always issued with a work and are considered an integral part of it.

Accompanying material. Guides, notes, leaflets, audio and visual material issued with the work to convey its concepts more completely.

Adaptation. A new version of a work frequently modified for a purpose or use other than that for which the original work was intended.

Added entry. An entry in addition to the main entry under which a work is represented in a catalog; a secondary entry which is a duplicate of the main entry or unit card with the heading for creator, subject, title, etc.

Alternative title. A second title introduced by "or" or its equivalent.

Analytical entry. The entry for a part of a work, or of an item contained in a collection of works.

Annotation. A note that describes or summarizes the content of a work.

Aperture card. A data card with a 35mm or 70mm microfilm insert. See MICROFORM.

Area. A major section of the catalog entry, e.g., the Imprint area.

Art original. The picture originally created by the artist. See PICTURE.

Art print. A printed reproduction of a work of art, generally issued without textual annotation. See PICTURE.

Art reproduction. A copy of an original work of art.

Artifact. Any object made or modified by man. See REALIA.

Audible signal. The tone, usually in an audiorecording, which indicates that the visual presentation should be advanced to the next frame or slide.

Audio accompaniment. A work in an audio medium that provides the sound for a visual.

Audiocard. A card containing printed pictures or words and a strip of audiotape along the bottom edge. See FLASH CARD.

Audiocartridge. A permanently encased single reel and audiotape which has the ends joined together to form a continuous loop that provides playback without rewinding. See AUDIORECORDING.

Audiocassette. A permanently encased audiotape that winds and rewinds from reel-to-reel. See AUDIORECORDING.

Audiocylinder. A sound recording on a cylinder. See AUDIORECORDING.

Audiodisc. A phonograph record. The sound is recorded in a continuous groove cut in the revolving surface by a stylus responding to sound vibrations. See AUDIORECORDING.

Audiopage. A sheet with visual information on one side and a magnetic coating capable of recording and playing back sound on the other side. See AUDIORECORDING.

AUDIORECORDING. A registration of sound vibrations on a material substance by mechanical or electronic means so that sound may be reproduced.

Audioroll. A roll of paper or other material containing a pattern of holes that actuate the sound producing devices. See AUDIORECORDING.

Audioslide. A slide which is mounted in a magnetically coated frame on which sound is recorded, or in a frame on which there is a short length of audiotape. An audioslide requires audioslide (often called Sound-on-slide) equipment for use. See SLIDE.

Audiotape. A plastic tape which is coated with magnetic particles on one surface in order to record and reproduce sound. See AUDIORECORDING.

Audiowire. Magnetized steel wire capable of recording and playing back sound. See AUDIORECORDING.

Author. The person or corporate body chiefly responsible for the creation of the intellectual or artistic content of a work.

Blurb. A brief summary of the content of a work.

Call number. The combination of numbers and letters which indicate the classification of a work and its location on the shelf.

Card. See FLASH CARD; MICROFORM.

Card catalog. An index on cards, usually by author, title, and subject, which also provides descriptive information, to the works in a library's collection.

Cartridge. A permanently encased single reel of film or tape which has the ends joined together to form a loop that provides playback without rewinding. See AUDIORECORDING; MACHINE-READABLE DATA FILE; MICROFORM: MOTION PICTURE; VIDEORECORDING.

Cartridge filmstrip. A permanently encased filmstrip which is threaded automatically in a cartridge filmstrip projector. See FILMSTRIP.

Cassette. A permanently encased film or tape that winds and rewinds from reel-to-reel. See AUDIORECORDING; MACHINE-READABLE DATA FILE; MICROFORM; MOTION PICTURE; VIDEORECORDING.

CHART. An opaque sheet exhibiting information in graphic or tabular form or by the use of contours, shapes, or figures.

Classification number. The number assigned to a subject in a system which groups works of the same or similar subjects together. See Basic Rule XI.C, p. 25.

Collation. The physical description of the work which guides the user in the selection of any equipment which may be necessary to utilize the material. See Basic Rule VIII, p. 19.

Color code. The use of color on catalog cards to indicate that the material is in a nonbook format or in a specific medium. The practice is *not recommended*. See Basic Rule XI.D3, p. 28.

Computer tape. See Digital tape.

Copyright date. The year the copyright for a work is registered. Copyright is designated on the work itself by the symbol "©"; on audiorecordings the symbol "℗" indicates copyright.

Contents note. When a work consists of a number of parts, each of which has a distinctive title, these titles are given in a Contents note. See Basic Rule X.I, p. 23.

Continuation card. Additional card(s) required to record all the information provided in the descriptive cataloging of a work.

Creator. The author, composer, photographer or other person(s) responsible for the intellectual or artistic content of a work.

Creator main entry. The basic entry in the catalog for which the heading is the name of the creator of a work. See Basic Rules IV.C1-3, p. 6.

Credits. A note giving the functions or contributions of individuals who have been major participants in the creation of a work. See Basic Rule X.G, p. 23.

Cylinder. A sound recording on a cylinder. See AUDIORECORDING.

Data file. A collection of related records that are treated as a unit and represented in such a way that they can be read and/or translated by a machine. See MACHINE-READABLE DATA FILE.

Data set. A term often used to designate a data file, even though its meaning may vary according to different operating systems. See MACHINE-READABLE DATA FILE.

Data set name. The title locally and arbitrarily assigned to a data file which, for cataloging purposes, is not considered a valid identifier. See MACHINE-READABLE DATA FILE.

Date. The year a work is copyrighted, produced, or released. See Basic Rules VII.C1-4, p. 17.

Descriptive material. The material accompanying a work, designed to assist in its presentation or understanding, such as guides, notes, etc. See Basic Rule X.C, p. 22.

Digital cassette. A storage medium for a machine-readable data file. A permanently encased magnetic plastic or metallic tape mounted reel-to-reel. See MACHINE-READABLE DATA FILE.

Digital disc. A storage medium for a machine-readable data file. The data are recorded on a series of concentric bands on both surfaces of the disc. See MACHINE-READABLE DATA FILE.

Digital tape. A storage medium for a machine-readable data file. The data are recorded on a magnetic plastic or metallic tape usually mounted on a reel. See MACHINE-READABLE DATA FILE.

DIORAMA. A three-dimensional representation of a scene.

Disc. A disc composed of a substance on which audio and/or visual signals, or machine-readable data may be recorded and played back. See AUDIORECORDING; MACHINE-READABLE DATA FILE; VIDEORECORDING.

Distributor. The organization which has exclusive national distribution rights for a work. See Basic Rule VII.B3, p. 16.

Edition. The whole number of copies of a work produced from the same master and issued at one time or at intervals. See Basic Rule VI, p. 14.

Educational level. The level of understanding or educational attainment for which a work is intended. See Basic Rule X.A, p. 21.

EIAJ-1. Electronics Industries Association of Japan Standard for ½ inch videotape reel recordings. Also called Japan Type 1 Standard. See VIDEORECORDING.

Exhibit. A collection of objects and materials arranged in a setting to convey a unified idea. See KIT.

Extension of physical description. A statement of the physical properties of a work which further the description given in the Collation, or designate special equipment required to use a work. See Basic Rule X.B, p. 21.

Felt board. See Flannel board.

Fiche. A sheet of film, usually 4 x 6 inches (105 x 148mm.) with image reduction sufficient to reproduce up to 208 pages per sheet. See MICROFORM.

Filmography. A list of films, usually arranged by subject.

Filmslip. A short filmstrip, usually in rigid format and without sound accompaniment. See FILMSTRIP.

FILMSTRIP. A roll of film on which there is a succession of still pictures intended for projection one at a time.

Flannel board. A display board covered with flannel, felt, or similar cloth to which pictured symbols backed with the same or a similar material adhere. See CHART.

Flannel board set. Symbols designed for use on a flannel board which form a chart when they are displayed. See CHART.

FLASH CARD. A card or other opaque material with words, numerals or pictures designed to be displayed briefly by hand or by mechanical device for the purpose of drill or recognition training.

Flip chart. A set of subject integrated charts hinged at the top which can be flipped in a progressive presentation. See CHART.

Frame. One of the successive pictures on a motion picture or filmstrip.

GAME. A set of materials designed for competitive play according to prescribed rules and intended for recreation or instruction.

General designator. See General Physical Form Designator.

General physical form designator (Medium designator). Indicates the general medium in which the work appears. See Basic Rule V.B1, p. 10.

GLOBE. A sphere upon which is depicted a map of the earth or of the heavens, showing the elements in their relative size and proper relationships.

Graph. A diagram using dots, bars, or lines to represent the interrelationship of two or more things. See CHART.

Hologram. A three-dimensional image usually produced by laser photography. See PICTURE.

Imprint. The area of the catalog entry which records information about the production or publication of a work. The elements in the Imprint are Place, Producer or Publisher/Sponsor/Distributor, and Date. See Basic Rules VII.A-C, p. 15.

Inaudible signal. The inaudible pulse on audiorecordings designed to accompany synchronized filmstrips and slide sets. The pulse activates the mechanism which advances the material through the projector.

Integram. A hologram of moving objects which may be viewed without laser illumination.

International Standard Bibliographic Description (Monographs) ISBD(M). Rules designed to implement the international use of bibliographic records of monographic publications. ISBD(M) specifies requirements for the description of printed non-serial publications, assigns an order to the elements of the description, and specifies a system of punctuation for that description. See Section II, Punctuation, p. 32, and Bibliography, p. 225.

Jacket. See Microjacket.

Kinescope. A motion picture photographed from a television screen and usually mounted on a reel. See MOTION PICTURE.

KIT. A collection of materials in one or more than one medium that are subject related and intended for use as a unit. See also Multimedia kit, Programed instruction kit, Laboratory kit.

Laboratory kit. A collection of items or materials which may be in only one medium, intended for a special purpose, such as use in a laboratory. See KIT.

Lantern slide. An image, glass mounted, on film or other transparent material, 3¼ x 4 inches (8 x 10 cm.), intended for projection. See SLIDE.

Logical record. A single unit of information consisting of one or more fields of variables. See MACHINE-READABLE DATA FILE.

Loop. A short length of film, or audiotape or videotape, with the ends joined together in a continuous loop that provides playback without rewinding. See AUDIORECORDING; MOTION PICTURE; VIDEORECORDING.

Machine Readable Cataloging (MARC). A format for the exchange of bibliographic records.

MACHINE-READABLE DATA FILE. A collection of related records that are treated as a unit and represented in such a way that they can be read and/or translated by a machine.

Magnetic Board. A sheet of metal to which objects may be attached by means of magnets. See CHART.

Magnetic board set. A collection of magnetized objects that make a chart when they are placed on a magnetic board. See CHART.

Main entry. The basic catalog entry giving all the information necessary for the complete identification of a work, including the tracings of all secondary headings under which a work is entered in the catalog. The heading chosen for the main entry may be a personal or corporate name, or a title. See Basic Rules IV.A-C, p. 4.

MAP. A representation, usually on a flat surface, of areas of the earth or of the heavens.

MARC. See Machine Readable Cataloging (MARC).

Matrix number. The number assigned to the master from which an audiorecording is produced. Used only when the producer's serial identification number is lacking. See AUDIORECORDING.

Meaningless title. A title which by itself has no precise meaning. To make it meaningful it may be recorded in conjunction with a series title or be expanded by the use of additional words supplied by the cataloger. See Basic Rule V.A5, p. 8.

Media code. A two digit alpha code designed to facilitate the storage and retrieval of bibliographic and statistical records. See Basic Rules XI.D1-3, p. 26.

Medium designator. The term which identifies the basic or general physical format of a work. See General Physical Form Designator, and Basic Rule V.B1, p. 10.

Metric measurement. Metric measurement is preferred, but until the conversion is well understood, the size of tapes, reels, discs and slides, and audiotape playback speeds, is shown in inches. The metric measurement may be noted in parentheses after the measurement in inches. See Metric Equivalents, Appendix V, p. 224.

Microcard. A trade name for microimages printed on a card(s). See MICROFORM.

Microfiche. See Fiche; MICROFORM.

Microfilm. Microimages on film requiring a reading device that employs transmitted light and magnifies the images. See MICROFORM.

MICROFORM. A reproduction, greatly reduced in size, of alphanumeric or graphic material.

Microjacket. A plastic jacket containing strips of microfilm. See MICROFORM.

Micro-opaque. Microimages printed on opaque stock requiring a reading device that employs reflected light and magnifies the images. See MICROFORM.

Microprint. A trade name for microimages printed on sheets of card stock.

Microscope slide. A slide, usually made of glass, designed to permit the examination of an object through a microscope or microprojector. See SLIDE.

Mock-up. A representation of a device or process which may be modified for training or analysis to emphasize a particular part or function. See MODEL.

MODEL. A three-dimensional representation of a real thing in the exact size of the original or to scale.

MOTION PICTURE. A series of still pictures on film, with or without sound, designed to be projected in rapid succession to produce the optical effect of motion.

Multi-media kit. A collection of subject related materials in more than one medium intended for use as a unit. No one medium is so clearly dominant that the others are dependent or accompanying. See KIT.

Notes. Supplementary information given in the catalog entry about the nature and scope of a work, and any relationships not brought out in the formal description. See Basic Rules X.A-I, p. 21.

Open entry. A catalog entry which provides for the addition of information about a work for which the library does not have complete information or a complete set, or about a work of continuing publication, such as a serial.

Overhead transparency. See TRANSPARENCY.

Page. See Audiopage.

Phonodisc. See AUDIORECORDING.

Phonograph record. See AUDIORECORDING.

Phonorecord. See AUDIORECORDING.

Photograph. An image produced on a sensitized surface by the action of light. See PICTURE.

Physical description. See Collation; Extension of Physical Description; Basic Rules VIII, p. 19, X.B, p. 21.

PICTURE. A representation made on opaque material by drawing, painting, photography, or other techniques of graphic art.

Post card. See PICTURE.

Poster. A large illustration designed for display. See PICTURE.

Producer. The company, institution, organization or individual who determines the content and form of the material, and is responsible for its manufacture or production. See Basic Rules VII.B1-4, p. 16.

Producer's data. Catalogs, guides and promotional brochures issued by the producer, publisher and/or distributor.

Producer's serial number. The identification number which appears on an audiorecording and/or on an album. See AUDIORECORDING.

Production date. Interpreted as the date of copyright unless both a copyright date and a production date appear on the work itself, indicating that the production was completed but made available to the public at a date other than that of the copyright. See Basic Rules VII.C1-4, p. 17.

Program file. A machine-readable data file which contains the instructions that control the operation of the computer so that it performs the task required to produce the desired result. See MACHINE-READABLE DATA FILE.

Programed learning. See Programed instruction kit.

Programed instruction kit. A sequential presentation of material on a given subject designed to lead the user step-by-step to an understanding of the subject. See KIT.

Punched card. A storage medium for a machine-readable data file. A data card with holes punched in a particular position each with its own signification and designed to be read and/or translated by machine. See MACHINE-READABLE DATA FILE.

Punched paper tape. A storage medium for a machine-readable data file. Paper tape with holes punched in a particular position each with its own signification and designed to be used and/or translated by machine. See MACHINE-READABLE DATA FILE.

Puzzle. A work which presents a problem that requires solution, and tests problem-solving skills. See GAME.

REALIA. Real things as they are, without alteration.

Reel. A tape or film mounted on an open reel, and designed to play from reel-to-reel. See AUDIORECORDING; MICROFORM; MACHINE-READABLE DATA FILE; MOTION PICTURE; VIDEORECORDING.

Related works. Other works upon which a work depends for its intellectual or artistic content. See Basic Rule X.F, p. 22.

Release date. The year a work becomes available for wide distribution. See Basic Rules VII.C1-4, p. 17.

Relief chart. A chart which presents graphic information in a raised or three-dimensional form. See CHART.

Relief globe. A globe which shows the contours of the earth or of the planets in raised surfaces. See GLOBE.

Relief map. A map which shows the contours of the earth or of the planets in raised surfaces. See MAP.

Reproduction. An exact reproduction of a work in a medium other than that of the original.

SAN. Standard Account Number. See p. 28.

See reference. A direction from one term not used to one which is used in the catalog or glossary.

Serial identification (Audiorecording). The serial number assigned by the producer to identify the work. See AUDIORECORDING IV.B, p. 5.

Series. A group of separate works, numbered or unnumbered, usually related to one another by subject or content and bearing a collective title. See Basic Rules IX.A-B, p. 20.

Series title main entry. The title of a series chosen as the heading for the basic catalog entry. See Basic Rules IV.B1-3, p. 5.

Set. A group of separate works, numbered or unnumbered, which are related to each other by content, and the fact that each bears a collective title. The term "set" is often used interchangeably by producers with the term "series." See Basic Rules IX.A-B, p. 20.

Shelf number. The number assigned to a shelf in a fixed location system.

Silent filmstrip. A filmstrip produced with captions printed on the frame, or without captions and accompanied by a printed script. Such a filmstrip has no audio accompaniment. See FILMSTRIP.

Simulation. A work which presents a model of a real situation that requires role-playing and interaction from the players. See GAME.

SLIDE. An image, usually photographic, on film, glass or other transparent material, intended for projection.

Sound filmstrip. A filmstrip with sound track usually recorded separately on a disc or tape. See FILMSTRIP.

Sound page. A trade name for Audiopage. See AUDIORECORDING.

Specific designator. See Specific physical form designator.

Specific physical form designator (Specific designator). The term used to further refine the physical characteristics and functions of the medium of a work. See Basic Rule V.B2, p. 10.

Specimen. A part or aspect of some item that is a typical sample of the character of others in its same class or group. See REALIA.

Sponsor. The company, institution, organization or individual other than the producer who finances the production of the material. Sponsorship often involves the promotion, directly or indirectly, of a product or point of view. See Basic Rule VII.B2, p. 16.

Standard Account Number (SAN). A 7-digit code for the identification of bookdealers, libraries, schools and school systems. A 4-digit suffix can be added to identify branches and/or divisions.

Stereograph. A pair of pictures presented to give a three-dimensional effect when viewed through a stereoscope. See PICTURE.

Stereoscope slide. A pair of photographic images mounted to give a three-dimensional effect when viewed through stereoscope equipment. See SLIDE.

Store. The storage medium for a machine-readable data file.

Study print. A picture, generally with accompanying text, prepared specifically for teaching purposes. See PICTURE.

Subject heading. The word or words used in the catalog to index the subject content of a work. See Basic Rule XI.B1, p. 24.

Subseries. A series or set which is a part of a more comprehensive series. See Basic Rules IX.B, p. 21.

Subtitle. A secondary or subordinate title which usually explains or supplements the title. See Basic Rule, V.A9, p. 9.

Summary. A brief and objective statement of the subject content of a work sufficient to guide the user in selection. See Basic Rule X.H, p. 23.

Supplied title. A title supplied by the cataloger and shown in square brackets when no authoritative title is found on a work or in reference sources. See Basic Rule V.A4, p. 8.

Tape. See MACHINE-READABLE DATA FILE.

Tape-cartridge filmstrip. A synchronized filmstrip and audiotape permanently encased together which is threaded automatically in a tape-cartridge filmstrip projector. See FILMSTRIP.

Tape recording. See AUDIORECORDING.

Title. The name of a work, including any alternative title or subtitle.

Title main entry. The title of a work chosen as the heading for the basic entry in the catalog. See Basic Rule IV.A, p. 4.

Title reference. An instruction in the catalog which directs the user from one title to another or to the creator of a work.

Tracings. A record of the subject and added entries made for a work. See Basic Rules XI.B1, 2, p. 24.

TRANSPARENCY. An image on transparent material designed to be used with an overhead projector or a light box.

U-Matic. A ¾ inch videotape cassette. See VIDEORECORDING.

Ultrafiche. A sheet of film, usually 4 x 6 inches (105 x 148mm) on which the images of the original are reduced 90 or more times. See MICROFORM.

Uniform title. The title under which a work was originally issued, or alternatively, the title by which a work is most often cited in the literature. See Basic Rule V.A7, p. 9 and AUDIORECORDING.

Unisette. An oversized audiocassette designed for quarter-inch tape which may be used manually or stored in an automatic retrieval system. See AUDIORECORDING.

Variant title. One of the variations in title which may appear on a work. See Basic Rule V.A3, p. 8.

Videocartridge. A permanently encased single reel of videotape which has the ends joined together to form a continuous loop. See VIDEORECORDING.

Videocassette. A permanently encased videotape that winds from reel-to-reel. See VIDEORECORDING.

Videodisc. A disc on which audio and/or video signals are recorded for playback through a television receiver. See VIDEORECORDING.

VIDEORECORDING. A transcription of audio and/or video signals recorded for playback through a television receiver.
Videotape. A magnetic tape upon which audio and/or video signals are recorded for playback through a television receiver. See VIDEORECORDING.

Wall chart. A chart designed to be displayed on the wall. See CHART.
Wall map. A map designed to be displayed on the wall. See MAP.
Wire. A magnetized wire capable of recording and playing back sound. See AUDIORECORDING.

Appendix III
ABBREVIATIONS

A .... Adult level material
AACR ...... *Anglo-American Cataloging Rules*
Approx. ..... Approximately
b&w .... Black & white
© .... Copyright symbol (see also ℗).
c .... Copyright
cm. .... Centimeter (0.3937 inch); centimeters
cmps. ...... Centimeters per second
Co. .... Company
col. .... Color; colored
comp. ...... Compiler
ed. .... Edition; editor
e.g. .... For example (Latin, *exempli gratia*)
EIAJ .... Electronics Industries Association of Japan
fps. .... Frames per second
fr. .... Frame
ft. .... Foot (32.5 cm.); feet
H .... High school level material
hr. .... Hour
i.e. .... That is (Latin, *id est*)
in. .... Inch (2.54 cm.); inches
ips. .... Inches per second
J .... Junior high level material
K .... Pre-school level material
m. .... Meter (39.37 in.); meters
MARC ...... Machine Readable Cataloging
MeSH ...... Medical Subject Headings; the list of subject descriptors used in *Index Medicus*.
MRDF ...... Machine-readable data file
mm. .... Millimeter; millimeters
mono. ...... Monophonic
no. .... Number

Ⓟ .... Copyright symbol for audiorecordings
p. .... Page; pages
P .... Primary level material
q.v. .... Which see (Latin, *quod vide*)
quad. .... Four-channel; quadraphonic
® .... Registered trademark
rev. ed. ..... Revised edition
rpm. .... Revolutions per minute
s. .... Side
SAN .... Standard Account Number
sd. .... Sound
sec. .... Second(s)
ser. .... Series added entry
si. .... Silent
s.l. .... Without place (Latin, *sine loco*), place of production/publication unknown
s.n. .... Without name (Latin, *sine nomine*), producer/publisher unknown
SN .... Standard Numbering
stereo ...... Stereophonic
t .... Used in tracings to indicate title added entry
t: contents .... Used in tracings to indicate title added entry for all titles listed in Contents note
viz. .... Namely (Latin, *videlicet*)

APPENDIX IV
U.S. POSTAL SERVICE STATE NAME ABBREVIATIONS*

Alabama	AL	Montana	MT
Alaska	AK	Nebraska	NB
Arizona	AZ	Nevada	NV
Arkansas	AR	New Hampshire	NH
California	CA	New Jersey	NJ
Colorado	CO	New Mexico	NM
Connecticut	CT	New York	NY
Delaware	DE	North Carolina	NC
District of Columbia	DC	North Dakota	ND
Florida	FL	Ohio	OH
Georgia	GA	Oklahoma	OK
Guam	GU	Oregon	OR
Hawaii	HI	Pennsylvania	PA
Idaho	ID	Puerto Rico	PR
Illinois	IL	Rhode Island	RI
Indiana	IN	South Carolina	SC
Iowa	IA	South Dakota	SD
Kansas	KS	Tennessee	TN
Kentucky	KY	Texas	TX
Louisiana	LA	Utah	UT
Maine	ME	Vermont	VT
Maryland	MD	Virginia	VA
Massachusettts	MA	Virgin Islands	VI
Michigan	MI	Washington	WA
Minnesota	MN	West Virginia	WV
Mississippi	MS	Wisconsin	WI
Missouri	MO	Wyoming	WY

APPENDIX V
METRIC EQUIVALENTS

1 inch	25.4 millimeters	0.03937 inch	1 millimeter
1 inch	2.54 centimeters	0.3937 inch	1 centimeter

*See footnote under Imprint, p. 15. For list of State abbreviations in AACR, see its Appendix III, F, p. 364.

APPENDIX VI
BIBLIOGRAPHY

American Library Association. Resources and Technical Services Division. Catalog Code Revision Committee. Subcommittee on Rules for Cataloging Machine-Readable Data Files. *Minutes, Reports, Position Papers*. Chicago: The Committee, 1972-1975. Typewritten.

Anglo-American Cataloging Rules, North American Text, ed. by C. Sumner Spaulding. Chicago: American Library Association, 1967.

Anglo-American Cataloging Rules, North American Text: Chapter 6, Separately Published Monographs. Chicago: American Library Association, 1974.

Association of College and Research Libraries. Audiovisual Committee. *Nonprint Media in Academic Libraries*, ed. by Pearce S. Grove. Chicago: American Library Association, 1974.

Croghan, Antony. *A Thesaurus-Classification for the Physical Forms of Non-Book Media*. London: The Author, 1970.

Dewey, Melvil. *Abridged Dewey Decimal Classification and Relative Index*. Edition 10. Lake Placid Club, NY: Forest Press of Lake Placid Club Education Foundation, 1970.

Eyre, John and Tonks, Peter. *Computers & Systems; an Introduction for Librarians*. London: Clive Bingley, 1971.

Grove, Pearce S., ed. *Nonprint Media Guidelines*. Nonprint Media Guidelines Task Force, 1973. Mimeographed.

Grove, Pearce S. and Clement, Evelyn, ed. *Bibliographic Control of Nonprint Media*. Chicago: American Library Association, 1972.

Hicks, Warren B. and Tillin, Alma M. *Developing Multi-Media Libraries*. New York: R. R. Bowker, 1970.

Hicks, Warren B. and Tillin, Alma M. *The Organization of Nonbook Materials in School Libraries*. Sacramento, CA: California State Department of Education, 1967.

International Federation of Library Associations. *ISBD(M)—International Standard Bibliographic Description for Monographic Publications*. 1st standard ed. London: IFLA Committee on Cataloguing, 1974.

Library Association. Media Cataloguing Rules Committee. *Non-Book Materials Cataloguing Rules*. London: National Council for Educational Technology with the Library Association, 1973.

Sears List of Subject Headings. 10th ed. Ed. by Barbara M. Westby. New York: H. W. Wilson, 1972.

Tillin, Alma M. *School Library Media Center Procedures*. Madison, WI: Demco Educational Corp., 1973.

U.S. Library of Congress: MARC Development Office. *Films, a MARC Format; Specifications for Magnetic Tapes Containing Records for Motion Pictures, Filmstrips, and Other Pictorial Media Intended for Projection*. Washington, DC: U.S. Government Printing Office, 1970, and *Addenda* 1-4, 1972-1973.

U.S. Library of Congress. *Library of Congress Subject Headings*. 8th ed. Washington, DC: U.S. Government Printing Office, 1975, and Supplements, 1973.

Weihs, Jean R., and others. *Nonbook Materials: the Organization of Integrated Collections*. 1st ed. Ottawa: Canadian Library Association, 1973.

APPENDIX VII
SUGGESTED DESIGNATORS AND CODING FOR PRINT MATERIALS

General Designator	Specific Designator	Code	
Book		BA	
	Abstract	BZ	A summary of a document, speech, statement, etc.
	Bibliography	BB	A list of works on a particular subject or by a particular author.
	Book	BK	A publication which is complete at the time it is issued; a monograph.
	Braille book	BX	A system of lettering used by the blind in which each character is represented by a series of raised dots.
	Catalog	BC	A list, usually alphabetical, of books or items.
	Dictionary	BD	A book containing a list of words with information about their meaning and use.
	Directory	BR	A book containing an alphabetical listing of names and selected information about each.
	Encyclopedia	BE	A book or set of books containing articles on all branches of knowledge or all aspects of one subject.

Fiction	BF	A class of literature of the imagination, usually in prose form.
Guidebook	BG	A book of information for travelers.
Handbook	BH	A book of instructions and information on a specific subject.
Index	BI	An alphabetical listing of names, places or topics and the page numbers in the book on which each appears.
Leaflet	BL	A sheet of small pages folded but not stitched.
Manuscript	BM	A document written by hand or in typescript form.
Pamphlet	BP	A nonperiodical publication of at least five but not more than 48 pages, exclusive of the cover pages.
Paperback	BQ	A book bound in a flexible paper cover, often an inexpensive edition of a hardcover book.
Statistics	BS	A book containing a collection of numerical facts and data.
Textbook	BT	A book used in instruction which contains the basic principles of a subject.
Yearbook	BY	A book published annually which contains information generally up-dated yearly.
Serial	UA	A publication issued in successive parts, usually at regular intervals and intended to be continued indefinitely.
Annual	UU	A serial publication issued once a year.
Journal	UJ	A newspaper or periodical containing reports of work carried on in a particular field.

Loose-leaf	UL	A serial publication revised, supplemented and indexed by means of replacement pages inserted in a loose-leaf binder.
Memoirs	UM	A narrative composed of personal experiences or a collection of reports on research or experiments made to a scientific or other learned society.
Newspaper	UN	A publication issued periodically, usually daily or weekly containing news, comments, features, photographs and advertising.
Numbered monographs	UB	A series of books issued with a collective title usually by a university or learned society.
Periodical	UP	A publication issued at regular intervals generally oftener than once a year, intended to be continued indefinitely.
Proceedings	UR	A published record of meetings, minutes of a society, etc.
Transactions	UT	Papers presented, discussions, etc. at a meeting of a society or association.

INDEX